Journeying

Reflections of a Woman Traveler

Ellen Boneparth

authorHOUSE®

AuthorHouse™
1663 Liberty Drive
Bloomington, IN 47403
www.authorhouse.com
Phone: 1-800-839-8640

First published by AuthorHouse 12/22/2010

ISBN: 978-1-4567-1349-2 (sc)
ISBN: 978-1-4567-1348-5 (e)

Printed in the United States of America

In Memoriam

To Jim Wilkinson, the best partner for travel
and the journey of life

Introduction

All my life I've been consumed by the desire to travel. A passion, obsession, or, maybe, a form of therapy? Most likely, all of those.

On the road, I've traveled alone, with my husband Jim, or with wonderful women's groups I organized and led. Through those groups, I've made connections with women from other countries. I've worked with them, studied their lives, joined their causes, become their colleague and friend. In *Journeying*, I share much of what I have learned about familiar and new countries, about women, and about the cities, islands, mountains, and villages where I have encountered them. In learning about

1

some of the world's women, I have learned a great deal about myself.

A bit about how and why I travel. That means telling some of my life story.

I grew up in Manhattan, luckily in a privileged milieu. On vacations my school friends often traveled with their parents to exotic countries or posh resorts. Unfortunately for me, my parents believed travel was only for adults. Hardly adventurous, they usually opted for golf vacations in Florida or quick jaunts to the Caribbean. I envied my friends' suntans in winter and their skiing adventures in Switzerland. At least, in summers, I went away to camp in Maine, which I adored – partly for the serene lake, roaring campfires, and easy camaraderie with other campers and partly to escape my controlling family. At camp, I was on my own.

So, imagine my surprise when my parents announced, after they had sent me to camp from age eight to fourteen, that for my fifteenth summer they were taking me on a grand tour of Europe. My mother and I would travel together for three weeks in Spain and Italy then meet my father on the French Riviera from where we would all go on to Paris. I was wildly excited about seeing the places I had studied in school. I was also worried how my parents would "manage" me on the trip, and even more importantly, how they, perpetually in conflict, would manage to get along with each other.

In retrospect, my first overseas journey was a success, or, put another way, I don't recall any family fireworks. I do remember my mother almost collapsing in 100 degree heat in Toledo, Spain, as, perspiring heavily, she pulled herself up underground steps from what was reputedly El Greco's studio. I can picture my father in a fancy dress suit at the Hotel de Paris Casino in Monte Carlo, cheerfully pocketing poker chips that were soon lost, to my great distress, on his next round of gambling. I still see my parents in St. Tropez, pacing the sand in front of their beach cabana, anxiously awaiting my return from having a lemonade with an Egyptian lad I met on the beach.

More than anything on that trip, I recall longing for a

boyfriend instead of my mother and father, especially when I threw coins in the Fontana di Trevi, made a visit with my mother to the romantic Tivoli fountains at Hadrian's villa, or dined with my parents in a charming restaurant in the village of Eze overlooking the Cote d'Azur. For a dreamy adolescent, it was a European tour that tragically lacked a love story.

I soon realized it was also a tour for well-heeled foreigners. We viewed renowned sights from glass-enclosed, air-conditioned tour buses, slept in feather beds at deluxe hotels, and dined on snails and roast duck at gourmet restaurants. Even at fifteen, I knew I wasn't learning a thing about the way "real" Europeans lived, thought, worked or played. Even then, I disliked packaged tourism.

When I was 17, I persuaded my parents to send me back to France for a "real life" European adventure – spending the summer with a French family. With a group of young Americans I set off on a program called the Experiment in International Living. I spent six marvelous weeks with a somewhat wacky family that lived in Belfort, a French town near the Swiss border. The day I arrived, I was greeted by my younger French "brother" standing on the roof of the house, wearing Napoleonic costume for my last name, Boneparth, and waving an American flag. It wasn't a Ritz Hotel, and I was thrilled.

At the end of the summer, I joined the other American students in my group and our French "siblings" for a camping trip in Provence. I finally satisfied my yearning for a European romance, falling madly in love with Pierre-Yves, my older French "brother" who was my "family" member on the trip. Rebellious teenagers, Pierre-Yves and I periodically left the group and took off on our own, much to the dismay of our faculty advisor. We explored Nimes and Avignon and some of the picturesque stone villages of Provence. I felt wonderfully daring and authentically French when, on a rented motorcycle, we zoomed past gesturing *flics* (police). I fell in love as we picnicked in the limestone mountains of Les Baux on crisp baguettes, soft brie and rough *vin ordinaire*. That summer, I relished living in another country rather than passing through as a tourist.

Since then, I have preferred to immerse myself in a new culture rather than see the world from a tour bus. Before setting off, I follow my own travel protocol. I absorb as much as I can from guidebooks, films and novels before setting off. I reside in one or two spots on my trip rather than constantly moving around. I avoid packaged tours and large chain hotels. I explore rather than sightsee.

I'm sure most travel fiends are motivated by the same things that drive me – curiosity, adventure, education. Yet, all those drives can be satisfied in other ways, such as taking a course, reading a book, or learning a new hobby. Choosing to go somewhere unknown, saving money and vacation days for a dream trip, setting off to discover other ways of life and traditions – these acts speak to a deeper longing.

To figure out my inner drive for travel, I had to take an honest look at myself. I've always been a restless person, changing careers, residences, lifestyles. My restlessness has also made me want to change locales. I quickly get tired of staying in the same place. Travel is one obvious cure for restlessness.

Travel is also, for me, an escape from routine. When I travel, my life pattern changes. At home I'm extremely organized. I plan my life, make lists and set schedules. I'm not that compulsive person when I travel. On the road, I leave behind the woman who orchestrates her days. I live in the present. Of course, I study bus and train schedules and work my way through guidebooks, but I also let things happen. Where I am at the moment, what new things I'm discovering – those feel far more important than fixed programs or plans for the future.

That explains why I especially love places where living for the moment is part of the national culture. I thrive in Greece and other countries in the Mediterranean where plans, if they are made at all, are easily altered and where pleasure is an expected part of any day. Letting go when I travel refreshes me; it shows me there are different ways to be.

Perhaps underneath my passion for travel, there is not just a desire but also a need. I suspect traveling helps me deal with depression. Over the years I have learned various ways to deal with it such as starting new projects or meeting new people, but those ways take time. For me, travel is an instant anti-depressant. I feel upbeat when devising itineraries, planning what to pack, riding on a plane, boat or train, encountering a new world. If my depressions were deep and chronic, I would probably bring them along in my suitcase. Fortunately, they are not, and, for me, nothing makes them more transient than buying an airplane ticket, grabbing my passport, and heading to an airport.

In the last thirty years, I've been absorbed by cultural studies, wanting to expand my mind rather than simply acquire stamps for my passport. Early in life, when my first husband and I were pursuing our graduate degrees and launching careers, we tempted fate by driving a rental car across the rugged, desolate Atlas Mountains from Agadir to Marrakesh or flying a four-seater plane from Cozumel to Chichen Itza over thick, unpopulated Yucatan jungles. Sadly, traveling was the only thing my ex-husband and I did well together.

At 27, I became a single woman again and was free to take off wherever, and pretty much whenever, I chose. As a university professor of political science and women's studies, I had long holiday vacations and summers. I suspect that freedom to travel was a major reason why, in my thirties and forties, I remained single and chose not to have children. Moreover, much of that time I found a way to travel expense-free.

In 1981, at 36, I created the International Women's Studies Institute (IWSI), a cross-cultural women's studies program that enabled me to lead participants of all ages to exotic destinations while simultaneously covering my travel expenses. From 1981 to 2009, I took the Institute to Greece, Turkey, Israel, Kenya, Hawaii, Australia, the Baltic States, Spain, Guatemala and Nepal. By studying women, we opened ourselves to realities previously ignored or misrepresented by male researchers and observers. On those women's studies journeys, I fashioned one way of creating global sisterhood.

In my late forties, I married again, this time to Jim Wilkinson, a man whom I knew would be the perfect travel partner. A career diplomat, Jim had lived and worked all over the globe. My trips with him in our retirement years included Southeast Asia, India, China, Australia, Spain, and Greece. While our journeys were incredibly rewarding, Jim, after a number of years, decided he was content to stay in one place he liked and found interesting, our home in Santa Rosa. That hardly described me. I was constantly fantasizing about my next voyage. For me, the best way to appreciate home was, for a short while, to leave it. Jim was willing to have me venture off, knowing I would always return home fulfilled and ready to enjoy domesticity – at least for a while.

I don't know what shape my future travels will take, especially now, after Jim passed away in 2010. I hope to find companions or groups that are compatible with my non-traditional travel style. Or, I may take off alone, even settle for a time in a new locale to experience more deeply an untried culture. There are so many possibilities.

There's only one thing I'm sure about – my suitcase will never get dusty.

Journeying has four parts, somewhat chronological but not precisely. In Part I, I explore Greece, a country I discovered in 1979 and have returned to over and over. In *Catching the Greek Spirit*, I describe how I first came to Greece and then to the island of Lesbos where I ended up becoming a godmother to my dear Katerina. An *Island Dream House* relates the experiences Jim and I had when we converted an abandoned olive press into our dream home. In *Longing Again for Greece*, I tell how, after selling the olive press, my first Greek island adventure, and traveling for several years to Asia and Australia, I still longed to live on a Greek island. In 2005, Jim and I returned to Lesbos to renovate an old, once Turkish home into a vacation place we ultimately gave to Katerina.

In Part II, I recount two journeys that helped me discover my heritage. In *Ilana, Welcome Home,* I set off in 1982 for a conference in Israel, a visit that unexpectedly struck a deep chord and pulled me back to Israel twice for extended stays. In *Baltic Roots*, I went on a "roots" trip to see the lands of Latvia and Lithuania and discovered the surprisingly wonderful Baltic states, links to my past although only indirectly to my own forebears.

Part III describes how women in several developing countries "hold up (more than) half the sky," as the Chinese put it. In *Indigenous Women Down Under*, I report on Aborigines in Australia. *Guatemala's Indigenous People* introduces the reader to indigenous Mayan women in Guatemala, survivors not only of crushing poverty and discrimination but also of a genocidal civil war.

In Asia, women's lives range from neglect in India to betterment in China to desperation in Nepal. In *Trying to Unravel India*, my experiences lead me to understand gender as an invisible caste. In *Gaping at China*, I witness women, along with their male partners, benefitting from the country's exploding prosperity. In *Women NGOs to the Rescue* I feature the roles played in Nepal by non-governmental organizations led by and benefitting women.

In Part IV, I explore new ways to travel. During our *Christmas with Sinterklaas,* Jim and I visit our god-daughter Katerina in Amsterdam and experience the joy of creating an overseas family holiday. In *Expats and Campesinas*, I go off to San Miguel de Allende, Mexico, and conclude that expat communities do not satisfy my travel instincts. In *The Costs of Volunteering*, I join a volunteer organization in the Cook Islands in the hope that helping out in a new culture will make a fulfilling adventure. *One for the Road,* based on coming to terms with the sudden and unexpected loss of my dear husband Jim, reflects on the challenges of traveling alone.

I have titled this book *Journeying* because, at its best, the experience of travel is more than taking a trip somewhere. A journey, according to Webster's, can be defined as a "passage from one place to another." Above all, that is what travel has been for me – a passage from ignorance to growing enlightenment. I came to see my community as stretching from my own hometown in California to villages in Greece, towns in the developing world, cities in Europe and Asia. More than anything, my travels have fed my curiosity and taught me compassion.

With this book I welcome you as a companion on my journey.

PART I

BONDING WITH GREECE

Catching the Greek Spirit

Over the years, curious friends have asked me how I became so intimately connected to Greece. They have wondered why I travel there so often, what about Greece has captured me. To casual acquaintances, I answered, "Sun and sea." Close friends wanted to know more.

"Did you study classics?" they asked.

"A bit," I said, "but I'm more intrigued by modern Greece than ancient."

"Do you have Greek blood?"

"Not at all."

"What is it, then?"

It's a question I've often asked myself.

Certainly, over more than thirty years, Greece has given me many gifts – two homes away from home, first in Aegina, then in Lesbos; exhilarating travels as a group leader; fascinating times as a U.S. diplomat in Athens; an extraordinary relationship with my Greek god-daughter. Yet, my attraction to the country is tied, in large part, to its spirit, in Greek, *edonismos*. Hedonism in Greece doesn't mean a desperate pursuit of sensuality. Rather, it conveys finding pleasure in the course of any day or evening, whether with family, friends or strangers. That pleasure can be as simple as wishing neighbors, co-workers, even people on the street, good morning.

Most Greeks believe something joyful will happen in the course of the day, if only they let it. They don't break into song or dance at the drop of a hat; they suffer as much as other people. But they pursue pleasure as a prime reason for living rather than as an occasional, lucky byproduct. I am invigorated by a place where kicking up my heels comes naturally and is appreciated. Greece has taught me another way to be.

The first time I visited the Mediterranean, I never imagined my tie to Greece would become deep and longstanding. In 1979, I set out for Europe with a boyfriend who had never been outside the U.S. He was anxious about every new and foreign thing – money, time differences, language, food, behavior. Throughout England and Holland, he depended on me to arrange everything. His contribution was to worry. By the time we arrived in Athens, our relationship was on its last legs. Still, it was my first time in Greece and I was determined to enjoy myself, with or without my companion.

Athens quickly seduced me as I gazed up to see the Acropolis towering above downtown. I savored Greek specialties in *tavernas*, fried calamari, salads piled with *feta* cheese, and carafes of *retsina* wine. I snapped my fingers to *bouzouki* music blaring from alleyways. Touring Crete was even better. My companion rented a motorbike and we cruised on curvy roads over tree-covered mountains. At roadside villages, we drank beer with old men in *cafeneions*. In one town, villagers in the square were roasting a huge lamb for their *panagyri*, the ultimate summer festival. That night of dancing and laughter made me forget my romantic troubles as I found pure pleasure in the moment.

The following summer I felt a strong urge to go back to Greece to experience everyday life and get to know the people. I convinced my dear friend Josephine to join me in a charming rental home on a picturesque Greek island. Alas, I had not actually located a rental. I hadn't even chosen an island. By the time we got to Greece and started searching, the inexpensive places we could afford had long since been reserved. Josephine was not happy with me.

We got as far as the island of Paros and rented a room at the harbor for a couple of nights. While we tried to figure out what to do next, by chance, or fate, we met an older American woman in a *taverna* who asked, "What are you two doing here?"

"Don't laugh," I said. "We're looking for the perfect house in which to spend the summer."

"I think we're too late," Josephine observed with a grimace.

"Not at all," Alda responded. "I have the perfect house. Come stay with me."

Alda lived in a hillside cottage in the middle of a vineyard. Her circular stone veranda was shaded by the branches of a magnificent frankincense tree. She gave us a free room overlooking the sea, and, in return, we helped her with chores she could not do because of health problems.

As much as I could, I immersed myself in the island lifestyle. I hung out with a group of fun-loving young Greeks who spear-fished all day and drank *ouzo* all night. I encountered a bunch of Americans who'd set up an art school that was accredited with numerous American universities. Their school planted a seed in my mind. I was a professor of political science and women's studies. Why not create my own travel-study program so I could come back to Greece every summer? I could put on a women's studics program in Greece. Although I had never heard of any such thing, I could innovate.

I wondered where to put my women's studies institute. Paros seemed logical since I already knew the island and had friends there. Still, there were many other possibilities. The next year, I came back to Greece to investigate. I went first to the island of Lesbos. I had read about the ancient poet, Sappho, who, in the sixth century B.C.E., had established a women's educational community in Lesbos. She had taught the arts – sensual and creative – to a gaggle of young, nubile women. I joked to friends that the lyrical poet Sappho, certainly the first women's studies professor in history, had spoken to me. Perhaps I would find my niche on her island.

I knew little about Lesbos, Greece's third largest island, except that it sat in the Eastern Aegean just off the Turkish coast. My destination was Molivos, a town known as an artist colony. On the bus from the airport, I quickly succumbed to the beauty of the island – rolling hills, rich in greens, from the forest green of pine trees to the silver green of olive orchards, and two-lane roads that, around each bend, offered startling views of the royal blue sea. The last five minutes of the bus ride were stunning. We crossed one more ridge, climbed a hill, and Molivos appeared in the distance, a hillside of stone houses graced with traditional wooden balconies perched above a glistening bay.

The bus dropped me at the foot of town. I had to shake off several local women, all in black, who were desperately trying to rent rooms in their homes to visitors. I trudged up the hill to town, a persistent landlady behind me who was tugging my arm. She almost secured me as a customer until she announced she would meet the next bus to find me a room-mate. I escaped her clutches and headed back toward the town square.

A handsome, dark-haired man, covered in automobile grease, lounged on the street. "You want a room? Private?" he said, his face, under bushy eyebrows, grinning widely.

"Yes, but no room-mate."

"I have room, same price."

I must have looked nervous because he said, "My wife show you. Good room. You see the sea."

I nodded reluctantly and he grabbed my duffel bag. I followed him to his own home and met his wife, who offered me a cold drink and place to sit and rest. This couple, Michalis and Nena Vatis, soon became friends, and eventually, a sort of family, although in a way I could never have anticipated.

Nena and I set off for my rented room. Their six-bedroom guest house was at the top of the village just below the huge stone castle. It was a tiring walk uphill, but I couldn't complain. Nena climbed the steep cobblestone streets in a skirt and high heels, my knapsack over her arm, while I, in jeans and sneakers, my hands free, struggled to keep up with her. When we reached her house, I was stunned by the view – a half moon bay dotted with a couple of green islands and a blood orange sun, balancing on a sheet of steel blue water. The double window in my room drew me like a magnet. During the five days I was there, I often sat in the window seat, absorbing a scene as close to paradise as I'd ever witnessed.

During my stay, Nena and Michalis included me in many of their activities – shopping in town, visiting a nearby beach, having a drink down at the harbor, meeting the extended family. I struggled to communicate, using primitive Greek and lots of hand motions. My mistakes were enjoyed thoroughly but I soon realized that if I wanted to embrace Greece fully, I would need to learn Modern Greek.

Molivos was trying to become a tourist attraction without losing its traditional character. The mayor had worked hard to maintain the architectural character of the town, which could best be called Anatolian or eastern Aegean. Its streets were cobblestone and only one allowed cars. The rest were narrow paths and alleys for strolling, many with stone steps. All the houses and shops were built in stone, with terra cotta tile roofs and bright crimson, blue or green wooden doors and shutters. Many of the restaurants had back balconies set with tables and chairs

Ellen Boneparth

that looked out toward the sea. My favorite fish *taverna* had a blackboard sign in front that claimed, no humor intended, "We have the best Lesbian fish."

In a few short days, I fell in love with Molivos. I decided to locate my women's studies institute there and rent Michalis' and Nena's house for students for the following summer.

That first summer, I brought 60 women's studies students, aged 25 to 60, and 12 faculty members to Molivos for a program that ran six weeks. I took on far more than I could handle. As the only administrator, I was responsible for every detail – course locations (often *tavernas* due to a lack of other meeting space), group meals, extracurricular activities, housing. I ran up and down the hill from the castle to the sea several times a day, losing 15 pounds without trying.

Nevertheless, the institute was a remarkable experience. Women from different ages and backgrounds built a sense of community. Our workshops – women in Greek philosophy and drama, gender in contemporary

Greek politics, interpretation of local women's stories – came alive. In costumes of white sheet togas, we even put on a play about Sappho for the village. I hoped, based on our successful program, that I'd be able return to Greece every summer for another institute.

The following year, my second institute did not start well. Upon arriving in Molivos, I discovered that, even though I had reserved Michalis' guest house months earlier, he had rented it to Germans. With an exhausted group of women students waiting at the bus stop, I scrambled around town to find six additional rooms for my group. Fortunately, over the winter, I had picked up enough Modern Greek to communicate about simple matters. Within an hour, I found a suitable rental, although lacking an entrancing view of the sea.

The next day I dropped in to see Nena, who was obviously embarrassed by Michalis' behavior. She apologized profusely. To my surprise, she was quite pregnant. The baby was due in a month. I quickly picked up on her excitement, and visited frequently to check on her condition. On one visit, Nena asked if I would like to be present at the birth of the new baby. I was thrilled, and scared. I knew nothing about childbirth except what I had seen in films. I imagined the process would be painful and bloody; it might even be dangerous. If I were asked to help, I wouldn't know what to do, especially if the doctor or nurse shouted instructions in Greek. Nena assured me that for her childbirth was easy. I suppressed my anxiety because I wanted to be there.

I came to see Nena regularly in order not to miss her delivery day, which would start with a 90-minute drive from Molivos to the clinic in the island's capital of Mytilini. One day, I had to go into Mytilini myself for errands and stopped by Nena's to see if I could pick up anything for her in town. I told her where I'd be all day in case the baby came early. She laughed at my excessive preparedness.

At 10:00 a.m., I left Molivos by bus, stopping off on the way to Mytilini at the old Turkish baths next to the Gulf of Gera. Just as I had eased myself into a steaming pool, the bath house matron came running toward me, shouting that the mother was being rushed by taxi to the maternity clinic. I tore out of the pool, begging the matron to call me a taxi. She insisted it would be faster to hitchhike. So, with a sopping head, I waved down a truck on the road. The driver, a swarthy Greek with a huge mustache, drove as if responding to a major emergency and delivered me straight to the small clinic.

By the time I arrived, Nena, in street clothes, was lying on a table, her spiked high heels flopped on the floor. No one else was around. I grabbed her hand, asked how she was feeling. Although in labor, she was in fine spirits. I was in a panic, wanting to know where the doctor was and why Nena had no hospital gown. Eventually, a doctor ambled in, took one look at Nena and prepared for delivery. Incredibly anxious, I clutched Nena's hand again. It was all over in fifteen minutes when a very pink, dark-haired little girl joined our company.

I was in shock. "So fast," I said to Nena. "How did you do that?"

She giggled. "I'm like a chicken laying eggs."

A half hour after delivery, Nena, her face cleansed by a wet towel, wanted to sit up. Although I urged her to stay in bed, the nurse encouraged her to move around. Nena hoisted herself up and looked for her shoes. She slipped on her high heels, and clutching me on one side and the nurse on the other, made her way to an armchair. Her new daughter was soon in her arms. The new baby would join an older sister and brother. I expressed my delight to Nena that "we" had had a girl.

Later in the afternoon, Michalis arrived to collect his wife, new daughter, and me. While pleased that everyone was fine, he was only remotely interested in the delivery, as if childbirth was just a mundane event. It was simply time to get home, and for him to begin providing for an even larger family.

A couple of days later when I went to see Nena and her new daughter, I discovered the baby had been born on Saint John's Day, June 23. In those days, the women of Molivos celebrated St. John's day as a kind of fertility festival. Married women built small fires in the streets and, chanting their wish for a new child, jumped over them. Likewise, young women wishing to get married observed St. John's Day by putting a ring in a glass of water overnight. The new baby's birth had been perfectly timed. She would evolve into a fertile woman – adventurous, creative, full of love and life.

On one of my visits, Nena surprised me by asking if I would like to be the baby's godmother, her *nona,* in Greek pronounced no-nah. I jumped at the opportunity, even though I knew nothing about god-parenting in Greece. I soon discovered that, in Greek Orthodox tradition, a godparent becomes a surrogate member of the family, a *koumbaros* or *koumbara*. The tie between the godparent and godchild's family becomes close and reciprocal. The godparent's duties include preparing the godchild for all major traditional celebrations, especially baptism and marriage, and reinforcing the child's affinity for the Greek Orthodox religion, a role for which I, a Jew, was not particularly well suited.

The godparent, especially the godmother, also has some special roles, such as helping choose the baby's name. I wanted a strong, feminist name and proposed Eleftheria, which means "freedom" in Greek. Unfortunately, the family didn't like Eleftheria, so I next proposed Sophia, meaning "wisdom." When the name of Sophia was also nixed, I felt frustrated. What I hadn't realized was that the family already had a name in mind, Katerina, for the baby's maternal grandmother. Innocently, I proceeded to suggest a last name, Margarita, in honor of Margaret Papandreou, an acquaintance of mine, a committed feminist, and the American-born wife of the Prime Minister, Andreas Papandreou.

Nena and Michalis said they loved the name Margarita, and I assumed we had named the baby Margarita Katerina. I promptly wrote Margarita Papandreou that the family was baptizing a child in her name and I invited her to the baptism the following June. Some time later, I found out the baby's name was actually reversed – Katerina Margarita. So much for godmotherly prerogatives.

I once asked my friend Nena why she had chosen me as a godmother.

She said, "You are woman who has done many things. You are free, you are a professor. You can help my daughter."

I was touched. I knew Nena led a traditional life – all family, cooking and housework. In summer she was busy preparing the family's rental rooms for tourists; in winter, she found a little time to pursue her passion for painting. She definitely had more modern ambitions for her children.

"Nena, I will help your daughter as much as I can, but I will be far away in America."

"You will find a way.".

And, as our lives unfolded, Nena proved to be a Greek Sybil who read the future.

On my last night in town, Nena and Michalis invited me for dinner down at the harbor. We ate barbecued octopus and drank local *retsina* under a full moon that cast pearly light on the sea. The evening was magical and, as I looked over at the baby, I felt touched to have been part of Katerina's beginning.

The following June, I was back in Molivos for another institute and for the big family event, the baby's baptism. Baptizing Katerina engendered even more anxiety for me than watching her arrive in the world. Choosing the baby's baptism outfit and a gold cross to bestow on her during the service was, for me, the easy, if somewhat expensive, part. In contrast, dealing with the crusty village priest, whose beard hung to his chest, was next to impossible. He disliked the idea of a foreign godmother and, when he found out I was Jewish, he completely resisted my involvement.

Quickly, we had to find a Greek Orthodox co-godmother. Fortunately, the local pharmacist, who shared my Greek name, Eleni, was agreeable. Next, the priest decided it would be blasphemous for a Jew to touch the New Testament during the service. There was no Old Testament in the village, so we started calling around the island, trying to find an appropriate scripture for me to swear on. We finally found an Old Testament in Mytilini.

Lastly, we had the matter of Margarita Papandreou. To my utter surprise, the Prime Minister's wife accepted my invitation to the baptism and arranged to come with a camera crew to film her "bonds" to the people of Greece. The Vatis family took the news of her visit calmly, at least ostensibly, never telling me they were aligned with the conservative party and opposed to the socialist Papandreous. Despite their political discomfort, they could not object to recognition for their baby daughter from the Prime Minister's wife. The news about Mrs. Papandreou's coming visit quickly spread.

By the day of the baptism, everyone in town who could possibly make it showed up at the tiny stone church, a huge crowd for an intimate setting. Fortunately, there was a patio where villagers could mill around. The baptism ceremony was terrifying. There was Margarita Papandreou with television camera lights bearing down, making an already hot day into a scorcher. Of course, she believed the baby was being named Margarita. There were Nena and Michalis, trying to be gracious, but not too friendly, given their politics. And there was the foreign *nona*, godmother, anxiously trying to remember her part in the service and staying as far away as possible from the hostile priest.

Somehow we got through it, with me, the infidel, handing the cross (which I was not supposed to touch) to the Orthodox *nona,* who slipped it around the shrieking baby's neck. Oddly, when the baby was dunked in the barrel of baptismal water, she calmed down. I kept telling myself during the ceremony the fuss was worth it, that someday little Katerina Margarita would have a great story to tell. Of course, in front of Mrs. Papandreou, we kept referring to the baby only as Margarita. All in all, I was a relieved godmother when we departed the church and set off for a family celebration at a restaurant in town.

My first summers in Greece were among the easiest and most fulfilling times of my life. Every day I sunned, swam in the Aegean, ate lunch and dinner out at an inexpensive *taverna*. My language skills were primitive, but "village" Greek got me by. Best of all, Greece gave me the joy of god-parenting, of playing a role in a child's life when I had no children of my own. At first, when Katerina was still a young child, being a godmother was rather like being a holiday gift-giver. I didn't know it then, but, ultimately, it became a meaningful – surrogate – motherhood.

In those first years, I never thought I would be connected to Greece for the next thirty. It was enough to know I could return in summers. I wandered all over the islands, made new friends in *tavernas* and *cafeneions*, shared my love of the country with women in my institutes. It was a world full of spontaneity and discovery. From the beginning, Greece taught me to allow room for joy in daily living.

An Island Dream House

After five years of spending my summers in the Mediterranean, I made a major career change in 1984, leaving university life to become a diplomat in the U.S. Foreign Service. With considerable persistence on my part, I managed to wangle a posting to Greece as my first overseas assignment. I spent four years, from 1986 to 1989, at the U.S. Embassy in Athens working as a political officer. It was an opportunity to get to know Greek politics quite well, which was exhilarating but nothing like my joyous summers of sun and sea.

To escape cold, dank Athens in wintertime, I rented a small flat on the island of Aegina, just a half hour's hydrofoil ride from Piraeus harbor. Aegina was another world. In the middle of the Saronic Gulf, it seemed immune from the stormy weather circling around it. My greatest pleasure on weekends was to leave Athens, bundled up in a heavy sweater and trench coat, and arrive at Aegina harbor with its lovely neo-classical buildings, where I stripped down to a tee shirt and sipped a cold beer in the sunshine.

After four years at the US Embassy, I took a Foreign Service posting in New York City at the U.S. Mission to the United Nations. I was sad about leaving Greece, but in New York I would be working with Jim, my future husband and a high-level U.S. diplomat whom I had first met when he came to Athens on State Department business. Within a year, we were making our lives together in Hawaii, where Jim became an adviser to the U.S. Pacific Command and I served as a Dean at the University of Hawaii in Hilo.

Hawaii was on the other side of the world from Greece. I was busy with a consuming academic job and a full-time relationship. I rarely thought about my Mediterranean days, at least at a conscious level. Unconsciously, I'm sure I compared my new island life on the rainy Big Island to the sun-drenched Greek islands, the calm, Pacific temperament to the effervescence of the Greek personality. Although both places were beautiful and atmospheric, they were radically different.

Jim suggested, once his divorce was finalized, that we get married. I was deeply in love with him, but found myself unprepared for marriage. It took me a while to figure out why. One evening, as we relaxed on our lanai, I made a confession.

"Dear, I've just had an unexpected insight," I said.

"What about?" Jim asked.

"My reluctance to get married."

He wrinkled his brow. "I guess you'd better tell me."

"I've been sitting here watching the ocean and the changing light. It hit me that I gave up Greece for you once when I moved to New York."

"So?" he pressed.

I took a deep breath. "I have this feeling that if we get married, I'll be giving it up a second time, that I'll never again live in Greece."

"Why not? Why couldn't we get married and live in Greece together?"

I was incredulous. "You'd be willing to live in Greece?"

"If that's what you really want."

"It would be my dream. Are you sure about Greece?"

"After I retire? Why not?"

Jim promised he would come to Greece with me, and Jim was a man who kept promises. I was deliriously happy. We began discussing marriage. At Thanksgiving, 1993, we held a wedding on our lanai that included our families, old friends from the East Coast, and many new friends from Hawaii. A month later Jim retired from the Foreign Service and I discovered I also wanted to be free. I felt an urge to find my dream house on a Greek island before Jim and I were too old to take on a house restoration. In 1994, I left my job and we set off for Greece.

Jim and I had no idea how to find my dream house. Like Odysseus traversing the Mediterranean, we crossed the sea to whichever island drew us. Fortunately, I had previously purchased a small apartment in Athens, so, unlike Odysseus, when we wearied of wandering, we had a home where we could rest.

Our first excursion was to the island of Evia, Greece's second largest island, northeast of Athens. In northern Evia I fell in love with a village called Wild Flowers (*Agriovotano*) which had a rustic wood cabin for sale that obviously needed a lot of work. While the prospect of making house repairs didn't faze us, there were few shops around for acquiring building supplies. Still, northern Evia seemed ideal until we made our drive back to Athens which took us close to five hours. The village of Wild Flowers was too remote. Strike One.

Our next house-hunting trip took us to the island of

Crete, even further from Athens than Evia, where an old friend was selling the neoclassical house in which he had grown up. He warned it needed repairs. That was Greek understatement. While the stone exterior appeared solid, plaster was falling everywhere inside, the wood beams had rotted, and a huge fig tree was growing placidly in the living room where the roof had collapsed. A primitive bathroom and kitchen stood in the backyard. Clearly, we would have had to do a top to bottom renovation. At the price my friend was asking, we could not afford both the house and reconstruction. Strike Two.

By then, I knew I wanted to be close to Athens, which was why I never considered buying in Lesbos. As much as I loved Sappho's island, I didn't want to be a plane trip or overnight ferry ride away from Athens. Of course, I had misgivings about not being close to my god-daughter in Lesbos, but it was far more practical to settle down a short distance from the Athenian friends I'd known in my Embassy years. Jim agreed.

Our desire for proximity led us back to Aegina, my

island escape during my years at the Embassy. Friends there urged us to consider a great buy – the village olive press. They didn't prepare us at all for what we found – a small, dilapidated building from the 1880s that had been abandoned in 1960 when the last owner died. The exterior did not make a good impression – the press had yard-thick stone walls, but also a broken roof of cracked or missing terra cotta tiles. Inside was worse. Oil-pressing equipment, tools, and pieces of century-old paraphernalia were scattered about on a dirt floor covered by crushed olive pits.

Jim and I climbed through the broken wooden slats of the front door into the dark main room, wrinkling our noses at strong odors of rust and decay. Gradually, as our eyes adjusted to the gloom, we discerned, through shafts of daylight, a large circular basin of stone with a round, five foot tall millstone standing inside it. A long piece of wood, apparently the lever used to roll the stone around the basin, extended from the millstone's center. From the saddle and blinders on the wall we guessed that a donkey, tied to the lever, had pulled the millstone around the pit.

On one side of the room stood a rusted iron screw press surrounded by battered metal pails and pitchers cast off onto the ground. Two waist-high, clay oil jugs, or *amphora*, lay on their sides. On the opposite side of the room sat an open stone oven. Next to it was a second round structure that turned out to be the collar of a clay cistern dug many meters into the ground. Although the room looked nothing like my fantasy dream house, it felt like stepping into living history.

Jim and I crossed to an interior door and shoved it open. Behind it were two small rooms, probably for storage, that had deteriorated even more than the main room. The roof had collapsed, revealing a sky the color of robins' eggs. A large hole in the back wall gaped where there had once been a window. We walked over to the hole and looked out. I inhaled sharply. Before us was an extraordinary canvas – in the center, a huge expanse of dark blue sea, dotted with distant islands; below, rows of olive trees lining stone terraces; above, puffy cotton clouds. The view I'd always dreamed of.

On the way back to Athens, and for days afterward, Jim and I debated the virtues of the olive press. "It's historic," I claimed. "And the view is extraordinary."

"It is history," Jim said drily, "but turning history into a home with modern conveniences is not easy. By the time we pay for the renovation, we could buy a place twice the size."

"But it wouldn't be an olive press," I objected. "Anyway, I bet we can buy the press for a lot less than they are asking."

Jim bit his lip. "Even if we could do the place on our budget, it would be a bad investment. It needs everything."

"Would you at least come back to Aegina and talk to Stella, the architect I know there? We need a professional's input."

When Stella came to the village, she was entranced by

the press. I had known she would be since she loved old things. She urged us to buy it.

Several months later, Jim and I placed forty thousand dollars in cash into the hands of the seller. The restoration plan drawn up by Stella would cost at least that much. We began a search for workmen and were blessed by meeting Thanasis, a short, wiry, Greek-Albanian stonemason, who knew everything about building in stone and became a good friend.

Jim, who had many house-building skills, happily set up his carpentry shop in the yard. He never told me it was the first time he'd constructed doors and windows. To Jim, building projects were a matter of logic combined with trial and error. Every day he designed, cut wood, and fitted lumber into doorways and window openings. He made everything in traditional village style, including a donkey door that opened in mid-section to let light in and keep a donkey out if, of course, we'd had one.

In the first months we had to pick up Greek building vocabulary, accept that some days workers would just not show up, and deal with the stares of neighbors watching the Americans do much of the work themselves. The concept of "do it yourself" had not penetrated Greek culture. Manual labor was what workers, not homeowners, did. Our neighbors knew we had enough money to hire workers, so why was Jim carrying around stone and lumber and why was Ellen covered by varnish and paint? Villagers often gathered in front of our house, making friendly comments, then shaking their heads in dismay behind our backs.

To be fair, at the end, our friends and neighbors respected what we had done. They even brought strangers from across the island to see what they called a "museum." When we arranged our furniture in and around the oil-making equipment and tools, it looked like a pleasing nineteenth century factory with twentieth century decor. We were proud of the results.

Although restoring the olive press kept us extremely busy, I often thought about Lesbos and losing my connection to Katerina. I considered making a visit to

Molivos but felt awkward about suddenly dropping back into the Vatis family after a ten-year physical absence. I worried Katerina would have no interest in me. Why should she? I had been nothing more to her than holiday cards and gifts.

Looking back now, I realize I was also feeling shame. Katerina was now a teenager and I had contributed nothing to her process of growing up. Torn between my desire to show her affection and my fear of her rejection, I avoided disappointment by staying away. I was trying to protect myself, but actually hurt myself by not reconnecting.

One day, a conversation with an American friend who had settled in Molivos forced me to face my dilemma. My friend said, "You have to see your god-daughter. She's a lovely girl."

"I can't just drop in. The last time I saw her she was five. Now she's fifteen."

"Don't be silly," my friend said. "The family understands you were in America, but now that you're here..."

"They're going to be angry with me for ignoring Katerina. And what will *she* think?"

My friend sighed. "Villagers aren't like that. They'll be thrilled to see you. You can get to know Katerina *now* and be part of the rest of her life."

I decided, despite my anxiety, to go to Lesbos. Jim, who stayed behind to work on the olive press, pointed out to me that, at worst, a relationship with Katerina would simply not happen. At best, we might enjoy each other.

I stopped by Nena's home as soon as I arrived in Molivos. I gave Nena a big hug, then turned to face a slim, teenaged girl whose face was encircled by cascades of wavy, black hair. "*Yia sou, Nona*," she said and came over to give me a kiss. My heart bounced when I heard her say *Nona*. She reconnected without any hesitation. We proceeded to chat, a little in Greek, a little in English which she had been studying at school. Nena, Katerina and I made a date to have lunch at the beach the next day.

Our beach excursion was great fun. I swam with

Katerina who, tanned and diving forward and backward, frolicked like a sleek seal. I jokingly called her *fokaki,* little seal. I soon learned that being a seal in Greek is like being a cow in English. Still, Katerina gamely told me she'd try to get used to Fokaki. After a long lunch, Katerina went off to read a book on the beach rather than hang around with the adults. Good for her. My first impression was of an intelligent, independent girl with a great deal of maturity.

I saw Katerina a couple of other times before I left the island. Saying farewell, I asked her if she would like to visit Jim and me in Aegina the next summer. She was thrilled. I said we might arrange a few days of camping on the Peloponnesus. That made her intensely curious; she had never been camping and knew little about it. I realized it would be a joy to expose this delightful young woman to things she would not otherwise experience.

For quite a few years, the olive press was a dream house. I remember waking in the early hours, having coffee in the garden as the sun came up, reflecting on which garden plot I would work on that morning. Having been a city girl all my life, it was my first garden. It took me several years to realize I was better off planting native bushes and herbs like oleander, rosemary and lavender than the temperate clime roses and lilies I first put in.

Around noon, I usually hopped in the car and drove down the back side of the mountain to a beach few people visited. Often, during the week, I had the whole bay to myself and swam back and forth, parallel to the shore, feeling as if it were my own island. At the beach's *taverna*, often the only customer, I consumed a huge Greek salad, crowned with fresh capers, and drank a cold beer. I read, chatted with the woman *taverna* owner, or simply sat and stared contentedly at the sea.

In afternoons, to the buzz of crickets, I indulged in a nap, a habit I easily persuaded Jim to pick up. Our "mid-day sleep" (in Greek) became a lifelong habit. Then, in the late afternoon, we often took a walk. My favorite hike was up Mount Oros, which we could see from our garden, past wild olive trees, small boulders, and fields of purple thyme for a panoramic view of Aegina and the seas surrounding the island.

Once home, in the early evening, we brought some *feta*, local pistachios, and a flask of *retsina* up to our second floor veranda and watched the sun set over the Saronic Gulf, turning the sea copper, rose and violet. After dark, we'd have dinner in the olive press with baroque music on the sound system and all our restored treasures of oil-making equipment glowing around us.

It sounds perfect, and for some time it was. But, by our seventh summer in Aegina, I was feeling restless. I knew the island extremely well, perhaps too well, having driven, hiked or swum in most locations, having eaten in almost every restaurant, and having drunk coffee or *ouzo* in almost every cafe. I was tired not only of Aegina, but of Greece. I wanted to see other parts of the world.

My strongest personal tie to Greece – Katerina – was by then solidified. She was coming to California to go to junior college and would live with Jim and me. Having

Katerina in my life in such a profound way felt like I was bringing Greece home.

Jim and I began to think about selling the olive press and freeing ourselves for other journeys, but we did nothing about organizing a sale. When, early that summer, a couple came by to ask if we might sell, I politely said no, then went inside the house and, feeling ambivalent, cried at the thought of losing the house. At the end of the summer, another eager couple from Athens came by to ask about a sale. By that point, Jim and I had talked so much about selling that I was psychologically ready. The purchasers quickly agreed to our terms. We shook hands and, in what felt like an instant, the deal was done.

When I reflect today on my fantasy of finding my dream house, I realize it wasn't a house that I longed for but an escape to a magical place. When Greece became less alluring, at least for a time, than journeys elsewhere, the olive press ceased being my dream, and became someone else's.

Longing Again for Greece

After selling the olive press and making exhilarating journeys over several years to other countries, I once again felt my unquenchable longing for Greece. It hit me again in the spring of 2005 when Jim and I were living in Santa Rosa, California. I found myself waking in the morning feeling depressed. I had given up the one thing I'd always wanted, a Greek island home. I'd had my reasons and, underneath them, had been my perennial restlessness. Now I was grieving what I had lost.

One evening over dinner, I broached my feelings with Jim.

This time, a few years ago, I said mournfully, "We

would have been settling into the olive press for the summer."

"And repairing the damage from the winter. You always complained about all the work we had to do," he replied.

"That's true, but along with the work on the house came an incredible view of the sea, our fantastic home, days at the beach, dinners at *tavernas.*"

Jim played with his fork, then looked up. "And you want all that again."

I took a sip of wine and a deep breath. "Yes, I do."

He shook his head but smiled. "Then you'd better start looking around."

That was all it took. By then I had such a deep connection to Katerina, who had been with Jim and me in Santa Rosa for her college years, that I began imagining a house in Molivos. I asked my good friend Nena, Katerina's mother, to see what was available even though it would be a hassle to buy on Lesbos. For Americans, acquiring property on Greece's periphery, such as Lesbos which is just across from Turkey, required government permission. Then, cleverly, I got the idea of buying in Katerina's name. Since I was planning to leave her a portion of my estate when I died, why not a house for her to enjoy or rent out? At the same time, by using her name, Jim and I could avoid the Greek bureaucracy.

In July, I got an email from Katerina saying Nena had found us a place in Molivos! Katerina wrote the house had a lovely view of the sea but was '*kinda weirdly built.*' Evidently, the house was composed of three separate buildings, each containing one room. I didn't relish the idea of walking outside to the bathroom. Moreover, one of the buildings shared a common wall with neighbors. If they were noisy, that could mean a lot of problems. All that for over $100,000, I thought ironically. We kept looking.

Nena's next find involved a house costing twice as much. It had a fantastic location, sitting at the top of the hill just below the medieval castle. It was close to Nena's house where I had first rented a room in 1981 and fallen in love with Molivos. Katerina wrote excitedly, *"You can sit and see the sunset, and have the Aegean between your legs (Greek expression)."*

Unfortunately, not only did the second house start out at a high price, but the owners raised the price to $250,000, and much more would be needed for renovation. The price was a sign of those times – escalating property values, especially in beautiful towns like Molivos, and a market of Europeans willing to spend a lot for island homes. Katerina knew the house was way beyond our budget. *"Sorry for the ridiculous price,"* she wrote, *"I guess people are getting more and more greedy."*

Really wanting to plant roots in Lesbos, I came up with an alternative house-buying strategy. I suggested to Jim that we look in Vafios, the small village next to Molivos which sat on a hill five kilometers above the sea. The prices were much more reasonable there and I loved the idea of being in a village of Greeks with only a few foreign residents. Jim and I searched the Internet and, surprisingly, found a couple of Vafios houses for sale. We asked Nena to become our private detective. She looked and rejected both of the houses advertised online. On her own, she found another Greek "ruin," a stone house over a hundred years old, originally built by a Turk during the Ottoman occupation of Greece. It had a phenomenal view and a bit of land, but it needed much work.

Knowing how to appeal to me, Nena declared the house was "perfect for a writer." And the price, at $70,000, was lower than anything available in Molivos, although still high for a "ruin." I was immediately intrigued but feared that, as soon as the owners found out Americans were interested, the price would go up. I urged Nena to tell the owner she was considering the house for her daughter Katerina – a bit of a stretch, but with some truth to it.

The owner informed Nena some foreigners were interested in the house. Jim and I thought he was employing a sales tactic. Still, knowing real estate sometimes moves quickly in Greece, we decided to take a look before someone else snapped up the property. Jim was intrigued because the restoration job sounded a lot like our work on the olive press in Aegina and he was eager to resume his role as house restorer. We headed to Lesbos in October, and, the day after we arrived, we drove up to Vafios with Nena.

Not wanting to alert the villagers, we looked over the property quickly and quietly. The small two-storey house was in abysmal shape. The tile roof was on the verge of collapse. Stone had fallen off the walls in a few places, leaving holes to the outdoors, and the wood on the doors and windows was rotten. The building's ground floor was divided between a kitchen with an open wood oven and another area that was half sitting room, half wooden staircase, also rotting. We carefully climbed the rickety stairs to the second floor, also two small rooms, with no bathroom in sight on either floor. Like the olive press, restoration would require everything. That was the bad news.

The good news, the fabulous news, was the view. The house looked <u>down</u> on Molivos, giving us a bird's eye view of the castle crowning the town. Beyond the town was the huge sapphire bay framed by its crescent-shaped coast. And beyond Molivos, the Turkish coast loomed, mountainous, metallic green, seemingly invincible. Then and there I knew I would do whatever I could to make that dramatic, panoramic view my own.

At lunchtime, sitting at the harbor before a plate of grilled octopus and a Greek salad, Jim and I discussed the Vafios property. Since we'd already completed a major renovation at the olive press, we took the prospect of another top-to-bottom project calmly. That was a grave mistake. We had only a vague idea of what would be involved in this new job and no way to estimate costs. Nonetheless, we decided to move forward. Nena and Michalis had coffee with the owner to see if they could bargain about the price, but he refused to budge. After consulting us, they agreed with him and shook hands. After Jim and I left Greece, I began having panic attacks that our purchase would not go through. After all, the whole matter rested on a handshake.

Nena kept assuring me the handshake meant it was a done deal. Not convinced, I called from the U.S. every couple of weeks to find out how the paperwork was going. Nena's constant reply was *"siga, siga,"* slowly, slowly. I was never sure if that was her advice to me or a description of the process. When, in early December, she announced the papers were all signed, I felt as if a huge stone had rolled off my chest. "It's ours," I exclaimed, "and our Katerina's."

When Jim and I returned to Lesbos in the spring of 2006, we embarked on several agonizing weeks of hiring workmen – construction workers, plumber, roofer, electrician, carpenter – to begin structural repair. Carefully, we obtained several estimates for each job. Usually these were hand-scribbled numbers on a notepad. In an email to Katerina, who was then studying for her psychology masters degree in Amsterdam, I expressed frustration over the bidding process. She responded wisely, *"It must be hard to trust all those people there, but honestly there is no other option. It is hard to do your own research, so, unfortunately, you have to give in, and, in a way, change mentality."*

Although Katerina's advice was right on target, I found it unnerving to negotiate for a sizeable job on the basis of a casual conversation and some hand scribbles. When we finally had our team of workers in place with agreements they would work on the house over the summer, we left the island. I felt satisfied. Foolish me.

Back in Santa Rosa, I happily launched into making plans to go back to Greece in October. After an hour's phone conversation with an extremely conscientious airline agent, I managed to secure no-charge Frequent Flyer tickets. It would take four different flights to get from San Francisco to Athens, but the tickets were free! Once there, we would also save on housing expenses since, during our first two weeks, we would house-sit for a Molivos friend, and then move to a room Nena and Michalis rented to tourists in summertime but was unused in mid-October. We would still have some bills to pay – car rental, food, and round trip flights from Athens to Lesbos – but, all in all, we would be able to travel inexpensively. I was proud of my ingenious arrangements *before* we made the trip.

When Jim and I arrived in Molivos, we discovered it was election time for local officials. We were astonished that Nena, who had never shown much interest in politics, had agreed to be a candidate for the city council. Her party had persuaded her to run, claiming her popularity in town would help. A few other women had been council members, and I encouraged Nena to try. Every evening, she went to outlying villages in the district to listen to speeches given by her party's mayoral nominee. As election day approached, she busily distributed information door to door and urged people to vote for her slate. Unfortunately, in the runoff election, Nena's party lost.

I was impressed that Nena, who invested so much of her life in household duties, was willing to become a serious candidate. Until then, she had spent many evenings home by herself while Michalis went out to play cards with his buddies at a nearby *cafeneion*. That always bothered me – Nena, home alone. I hoped her taste of politics would stretch her horizons, but in the following year her mother died suddenly and she took on household responsibilities for her father as well as for her immediate family. Providing for family was Nena's chosen role and one I came to respect.

Then, Nena's oldest daughter and son-in-law moved back from Athens to Molivos with their new baby, and Nena, in traditional Greek fashion, became a full-time grandmother. I understood that my dear friend Nena would never evolve into a western-style independent woman, yet we would always share a special bond – our love and aspirations for Katerina.

For Jim and me, the best part of the election was that, following the Greek pattern of voting in one's home village, all of Nena's children came home to Molivos to vote. That included Katerina, who came from graduate school in Amsterdam on a ticket partially paid for by her mother's political party, a special form of Greek political patronage. I knew Katerina would be caught up with family and friends and working at the polls. To make sure we had some private time with her, Jim and I volunteered to pick her up at the Lesbos airport and bring her back to Molivos. For ninety minutes in the car, Katerina, Jim and I chatted non-stop about her graduate studies in psychology, her boyfriend, and her Amsterdam roommate, a woman from Surinam.

After we delivered Katerina to her parents, we did not see her for three days until we met for coffee just before she left. I would have loved more one-on-one time, but at least we were able to take her to "her" house as it was being restored. I hoped the house would someday become a magnet pulling Jim, Katerina and me even closer together.

Before we came back in October, Jim and I were convinced we would find a structure resembling the architectural design drawn by our civil engineer. Far from it. Thanasis, our contractor, failed to consult the paperwork we'd left him and put the stairway back in its original place rather than on the opposite wall. Once he had poured cement, the only remedy would have been cutting through new concrete. We ended up re-designing the stairway to make it turn ninety degrees halfway up. Our good fortune was that Michalis, Katerina's father and the village iron-monger, was able to make an attractive iron staircase in traditional style.

Jim and I began working with our other craftsmen, each of whom had his own distinctive manner. Costas, the tubby young carpenter from a nearby mountain village, always had to negotiate his prices. He would quote a price for a job and, in dismay, I would respond, "So much?" He would groan in despair and sadly say, "I can come down only 100 Euros." I would agree, and we would both be happy. Vassilis, the mustachioed plumber, had fair prices, but was always rushing around, squeezing us in between other jobs. Yiannis, the electrician did orderly work, but had to contend with the electric company which never announced beforehand when they were coming to the village to connect us to the system. I had to change my *persona* for every workman.

The enjoyable part of working on our "ruin" was becoming acquainted with our village. Climbing the side of a hill, Vafios was traversed by narrow, winding, cobblestone streets. Although it was possible to reach our house by car – and many workmen did maneuver their small trucks up to our parking space – Jim and I were reluctant to tackle slippery stones and sharp curves in our brand new rental car. Instead, we parked at the bottom of the hill and trudged up to the house, often laden with building supplies.

On the way up, according to Greek custom, we called out greetings to our neighbors who were usually sweeping their front steps or watering their plants. Many of the residents were pensioners who had spent most of their lives in the village. Down the hill from us were Maria and Frosso, two elderly, chubby sisters who lived next to each other and regularly invited us over for coffee. Across the street lived Anastasia, a cheerful, aging busybody, less than five feet tall, who came by every day to check on our progress. My favorite neighbor was Nikos, a rotund 82 year old, whose farm was just below our property and who brought us fruits and vegetables from his garden whenever he saw us. I ate more juicy, ruby red pomegranates that October than I had consumed in my entire life.

Above our house, up a stone stairway, stood the small village church and *cafeneion*, coffee bar, the former rarely visited, the latter receiving visitors all day. Another aging but lively woman, Vangeliki, served coffee and beer at oilcloth-covered tables outside, separated from her kitchen by a narrow village street. On rare occasions, we would have to get up from our outside table to make room for a car driving through.

To stay occupied, the old men made daily visits to the *cafeneion* where they sat for hours engaging in chitchat. The women, who came from a generation that rarely left the house, had television sets going throughout the day. Besides housework, gossiping on their front steps and visiting back and forth were their main daytime activities.

From my perspective, the village-bound people of Vafios seemed to lack external stimulation, but they were always lively and no one ever seemed lonely.

When our craftsmen finally finished their work, Jim and I were ready to launch our own building activities. After a heavy rain, Jim discovered humidity penetrating our thick stone walls. He set about building a cement apron around the house to stop water from seeping through the soil. He also painted our outdoor shutters and external doors a warm burgundy red. His most ambitious project was to build stone steps up to the tall mound of earth next to our house that would eventually be a garden. I had reservations about having Jim, then a man in his late sixties, lugging around heavy pieces of stone. He insisted and labored as a stonemason in between other chores.

My job was to stain the inside wood frames of our doors and windows a chestnut color. I started staining on a relatively warm day, opening windows and doors for fresh air and light. After three days, a fierce winter storm dropped temperatures to the thirties and forties. So much for my previous fantasy of a sunny, warm, building season. With no heat in our bulding, there was no way we could work in such cold weather.

During the worst of the cold wave, Jim and I stayed in the studio apartment loaned us by Nena and Michalis, out of town and right next to the sea. While the studio's location was delectable in summer, it was desolate in winter. The coast in front of the apartment was wide open. Across a large gulf, Turkey's gray-green hills stood tall against a billowing, charcoal sky. When the wind was blowing, as it usually was, we looked out on masses of whitecaps, or "little sheep" as the Greeks call them. The waves, which lapped softly in summer, thrashed the shore as if they might churn their way to our studio door.

To make matters worse, Jim and I were alone in the area, rather like being on an abandoned island. Two nearby hotels had closed for the winter. Vacationers had boarded up their houses and returned to Athens. Our only source of company was a fierce orange field cat and two kittens that hung around for food. Of course, once we started feeding them, they became extremely affectionate. Jim and I happily expanded our family size to five.

We burrowed in our room, reading, writing, and huddling next to our small space heaters. Living in our studio was a bit like camping. We had basic necessities such as a small refrigerator and hot plate, and our bathroom usually had solar-heated water. With one borrowed and one purchased floor heater, our room became comfortable after the heaters ran for an hour or so. We slept, barely able to move, under stacks of heavy Greek woolen blankets.

If Nena hadn't been a political candidate, we would have enjoyed meals with her and Michalis, but politics came before socializing. Fortunately, for entertainment, besides reading and writing, we had with us two addictive activities – a Scrabble set and playing cards for a Greek game called Biriba, halfway between gin rummy and canasta. Biriba is so absorbing that Greeks traditionally play on Christmas and New Year's Eve, starting at midnight and quitting at four or five in the morning!

What felt most like camping was our isolation from

the rest of the world. We lacked radio, television, English newspapers, a sound system, a land-line telephone, and the Internet. We coped by using a costly cell phone, reading Greek newspapers, and visiting, almost daily, an Internet café – a hole-in-the-wall with four slow computers, and a crowd of local men polluting the air with bitter cigarette smoke.

The wear and tear of working on the house and living less than comfortably "although, admittedly, better than ninety-nine percent of humanity" put some strain on our marital union. I kept trying to figure out ways to escape frigid Greece, but with non-refundable airplane tickets, any alteration in our itinerary would have been extremely expensive.

"Even if we can't go home early," I said to Jim, "we could go some place warm for ten days."

He looked skeptical. "Like where?"

"Egypt... or Morocco."

"If you"re willing to spend all that money, you might

as well pay to go home early. There's still a lot of work to do here. I want to finish up."

"I'd never let you stay here alone," I said. "Are you sure you wouldn't like to see Morocco?"

"Not high on my list," he said, grinning.

I had to appreciate Jim's unceasing good humor. During our whole time in Greece, he never once pointed out that I had arranged a six-week trip for a time period that turned cold and stormy. He hardly ever complained about the chill or lack of amenities. His patience convinced me to stop whining and tough it out.

When we finally left Vafios, our house looked a lot better. We had two bathrooms, one with a large bathtub, a handsome iron staircase, beige/rose tiled floors, chestnut-colored woodwork, and burgundy doors and shutters. In our next phase, we would paint the walls and ceilings white, get kitchen cabinets installed, buy and install furniture. And, in the future, we would do it the Greek way and go with the flow. Fixating on schedules, getting frustrated by tardy or careless workmen, counting on ideal weather conditions — these would get us nowhere. Whatever was meant to happen would happen.

Perhaps the greatest joy in doing the Vafios house was anticipating the pleasure it would eventually give Katerina. Jim and I hoped she would end up with a house that would be easily rented in the summer and would earn her supplemental income. We also wanted her to use the house herself sometimes and invite friends to come stay with her. Most of all, we hoped times would come when we three were there together, not for extensive holidays – the house was too small for that – but for short visits during which we would catch up on each others' lives.

My years in Greece brought me deep connections to two islands – Aegina and Lesbos. On both islands, Jim and I became deeply immersed in village life as we restored the olive press and then the old Turkish home in Vafios. Our years of carpentry, house painting, stone masonry and gardening made us members of a local community rather than merely vacationers. We loved digging deep into the earth of a new land.

With all of our experiences of island life, the one with the most meaning for me was shaping a friendship with a mother and daughter. Early on in my Greek years, Nena made me her companion and confidante, and godmother to Katerina. Nena admired me and chose me as a role model for Katerina. She might not be a "liberated" woman herself, but she found a way to gift her daughter with that through her godmother. The trust she placed in me, which never wavered despite years of distance, taught me a profound lesson. Despite our different nationalities, lifestyles and circumstances, the values we shared – openness, laughter, loyalty, curiosity about each other's lives – made us sisters.

My relationship with Katerina has been one of the great joys and best surprises of my life. I had chosen not to have my own children and never thought mothering was an experience I would want. Then, I came to love a Greek teenager who had a voracious taste for life and the ambition, intelligence and courage to make her dreams come true. She brought me and Jim into her maturation process as "second" parents.

Because I will always love Katerina and Nena, I will always love Greece. My future travels there may not be as frequent as in the past, but they will never cease.

Still, my restless spirit has always made me want to see more of the world than Greece. Over the next years, curiosity about my roots took me off on adventures that helped me better understand my heritage and place in the world.

PART II

SEEKING MY HERITAGE

Ilana, Welcome Home

As a young Jewish girl, I had little interest in Israel. None of my immediate family were Zionists. Rather, they were assimilated Jews whose interest in their religion went no farther than participating only occasionally in their reform synagogue and making social connections. Not only did I lack any desire to go to Israel, but I also knew very little about the country.

In 1981, when I was in my mid-thirties, long before I met Jim and just as I was discovering Greece, I was teaching political science and women's studies at San Jose State University. I decided to present a paper at an international women's conference in Haifa, Israel, because my university would pay part of my airfare and I could stop off in Athens on the way home and make some connections for my women's studies institute. On Christmas Day, I flew from California to Boston and then connected to a flight to Tel Aviv. I hoped I would have no one sitting next to me and would be able to curl up across two seats.

No such luck. A small man with darky wavy hair sat down next to me and introduced himself. He was also a university professor, the Chair of the Jewish Studies Department at Hebrew University. Given my ignorance about Judaism, I figured we'd have little to talk about. How wrong I was. My seat companion was fascinating, and we talked for hours about everything from ancient history to the founding of Israel to contemporary Middle East politics.

When I told the professor my family name had originally been Ben Porat, he told me the derivation. The name comes from the recounting of the twelve tribes in the Old Testament. Apparently, the tribe of Joseph is described as Ben Porat Yosef. In Hebrew Ben Porat means fruitful vine or bough and refers to Joseph being a fruitful son. My seat-mate went on to tell me that if I used the Hebrew version of my first name, Ilana, which means oak tree, I would have a beautiful Hebrew name, Ilana Ben Porat. Oak tree with a fruitful bough. That was a wonderful way to think of myself – strong, fertile, graceful – and, according to ancient meanings, it really was my name.

When we finally flew in over the coast of Israel, I was captivated by the azure water and long sandy coastline. As I stared down at this new land, the professor said to me, "Ilana, you've come five thousand years and ten thousand miles. Welcome home." I was someone who, before that flight, had had no feelings about Israel, yet I began to cry.

I had planned to spend a week at the women's conference, but on the second day after I delivered my paper, I left Haifa for Jerusalem, determined to use my short time in Israel to explore whatever the spiritual and historical capital had to offer. As the bus climbed and climbed from the seashore up into the hills, I felt as if I were going into another world. In a way, I was. I later learned that making *aliya,* the Hebrew term for emigrating to Israel, literally means going up, as in going up to Jerusalem. A mystical place for Jews, Christians, and Muslims, Jerusalem is a city of meanings and symbols like no other.

Once there, I settled into the YMCA, a pleasant, inexpensive hotel right across from the elegant King David Hotel. On sightseeing tours, I visited the Old City, the Knesset and the Israel Museum, full of stunning archeological finds and art. The city's buildings, constructed out of Jerusalem stone, limestone in shades of pink, gold and sand, made the city seem woven together (which it certainly isn't) and inviting.

I was incredibly moved by Yad Vashem, the Israeli memorial to the Holocaust. Although none of my relatives were victims since my family emigrated from Eastern Europe to the U.S. long before Hitler, the reality of the

Holocaust hit me in the gut. I was confounded not only by the reality of genocide, but also by the historical power of anti-Semitism that culminated in Nazism. I cried when I saw the exhibit of gold stars worn by Jews in almost every country in Europe. At the same time, the garden and trees dedicated to the Righteous Gentiles who saved Jews during the Holocaust struck me as a healing,way to commemorate survival as well as loss.

My week-long exploration of Israel focused as much on the modern state as on ancient finds and narratives. Loving ethnic markets, I wandered around the Mahane Yehuda outdoor market where, despite warnings from shop owners with black beards and jet black eyes that the dishes were very spicy, I devoured Moroccan food full of hot chilies. It was fascinating to meet market vendors who exemplified Middle Eastern tradition, yet were Jews.

Addicted to warm weather, I made an excursion to Jericho, below sea level and deliciously balmy, where I visited the ancient walls where Joshua allegedly "fit" the battle of Jericho. I stuffed myself on pita bread and *babaghanoush,* eggplant salad at Arab restaurants. I was in Israel before the *intifadas* broke out and, with free access to the Occupied Territories, I eagerly wandered around Palestinian lands such as the Arab Quarter of the Old City and the West Bank. In some strange way, I felt as much a Semite as a Jew, ethnically, more than religiously, identified with the land.

One day, again out of curiosity, I took a walking tour of Mea Sharim, the ultra-Orthodox section of the city. No group of people could have been further from my own experience as an assimilated Reform Jew. The women were covered from head to toe with dark scarves over their heads, blouses to their wrists, long skirts and thick stockings. I wanted to speak with some of them about their lives, but our guide, a tall, gray-haired American, informed me the people of Mea Sharim resented tourists and the women were forbidden from speaking to strangers.

I had started out the tour with little understanding of the ultra-Orthodox. My feminist soul was shattered. Nonetheless, my sensitive tour guide, an American who had made *aliyah*, persuaded me that, despite my personal aversion to orthodoxy, Israel should be a place for all kinds of Jews. I came to see that for many Israel was far more than a response to the Holocaust. For the ultra-Orthodox, its meaning was ancient, Biblical, and living tradition.

The guide, Jacob, close to twenty years older than I, invited me to lunch, then dinner, and a relationship, educational and romantic, began. When, a couple of days later, my departure for Athens was scheduled, I was crushed about leaving Jerusalem. To my great delight, the airport personnel in Athens went on strike and my departure was delayed – one day, two days, three. My romance blossomed even more when I stayed with Jacob, who was separated from his wife, in the atmospheric and breathtaking nineteenth century hotel, the American Colony. The lobby has stone arches everywhere, intricate colored tile work, swaying palms, a courtyard with a fountain, and upstairs we had an exquisite room decorated with Arab fabrics and art.

I saw even more of Jerusalem in the next three days,

walking to different quarters with my new friend. Hearing Jacob recite ancient or modern history, eating Arab soups and pastries, catching the sunset on top of the city walls, all these made the romance feel deeper than a mere flirtation. When I finally left for Athens, I was in love, perhaps even more with the city than with my charming tour guide. That was a good thing since I regretfully found out by letter that he had gone back to his wife.

When I got back to California, there was a surprising message waiting for me from a woman political scientist I had met at the Haifa women's conference. She invited me to teach the first course on Women and Politics in the university's brand new women's studies program. I was thrilled. Once arrangements were worked out, I applied for a leave of absence from San Jose State for September, 1983. Eventually, I made contact with a young American woman who wanted to rent her apartment in Jerusalem. I was again off to Israel!

Beit Hakerem, the Jerusalem neighborhood I moved into, was an attractive leafy area west of the city center with moderate-sized apartment buildings. My building was at the bottom of a hill next to a wadi, which I soon learned meant an open field between two hills. On the rise, across the wadi from me was the Givat Ram campus of Hebrew University, to which I could easily have walked, but my teaching assignment was at the Mount Scopus campus on the eastern side of town. So, in the early mornings, I strolled the wadi, studying wild grasses and colorful rocks – a bit of the desert in the heart of the city – then climbed the hill to catch a bus over to Mount Scopus. It was a commute worth making, given the beauty of the Mount Scopus campus, constructed out of Jerusalem stone and looking out over the stark hills and Arab villages of the West Bank.

My women's studies class, taught in English, was composed of Israeli students fluent in English and a number of Hebrew University foreign students, mostly Americans. It was exciting to teach something that had never been taught in Israel and challenging to adapt my syllabus for Israelis as well as foreigners. I enjoyed going for coffee with my students to the noisy cafeteria and snacking on tasty coffee cakes, but I was embarrassed several times when I left my book bag unattended, a serious violation of security rules for which I was loudly chastened by a student security guard. My students told me that, over time, I would get used to Israeli security checks and rules, but I was always a bit on edge by the need for guards and strict rules in such a seemingly normal setting.

During my stay, my goal, in addition to teaching, was to learn some Hebrew. The traditional way is to attend a Hebrew school, *ulpan*, but the *ulpan*'s class schedule took up much of the day, every day. Unwilling to give up so much time, I looked around for a Hebrew teacher who might come to my house a couple of times a week to tutor me. By chance, over a cigarette outside the university library, I met a male graduate student who lived in my neighborhood and was eager to make some money by giving me lessons.

We studied together for several weeks before my teacher casually said something about being an Israeli

Arab. I was completely surprised and asked why he hadn't told me – not that it mattered except for my feeling so ignorant. He was equally amazed I hadn't realized that his name, Moin, was Arabic, but I was such a newcomer in Israel that names of all kinds were a mystery. We laughed and continued our lessons in Hebrew until I scheduled a trip to Egypt, at which time Moin taught me some Arabic. Quite honestly, he told me, I lacked a facility for either language.

Living in Jerusalem was harder than I'd expected because of my lonely weekends. The town shut down on the Sabbath as people, whether religious or secular, gathered to eat Shabbat dinner. For secular Jews, as all my friends were, Shabbat was not as much a religious practice as a family dinner. Unfortunately for me, there was no public transportation on Shabbat, also no café life, movies or entertainment. Occasionally, I was invited to join acquaintances for a Shabbat dinner, but lacking a car, I had to depend on my hosts for transportation and often felt awkward imposing.

I realized the best way for me to fill my weekend time was to travel around Israel. The Society for the Protection of Nature in Israel offered frequent, reasonably priced, excursions around the country. My first excursion was to the Negev, a trip that sparked my infatuation with the desert. I loved the subtle earth tones, the wind-sculpted rocks, the curious succulent plants that survived on so little moisture. I relished sitting on a boulder in dry heat to soak up the sun or cooling off in a breeze blowing across red, yellow, pink and ochre canyons. Most of all, I was entranced by the vastness, by feeling so small among the natural formations of the world. For me, the desert is even more mystifying than the starry universe because the desert, for all its vastness, has become a home for many peoples.

My trip to Eilat had an even stronger impact. I had snorkeled previously, but the Caribbean and Hawaii are pastel paintings compared to the stunning underwater canvas of the Red Sea. The Gulf of Eilat, or Akaba, depending whether you're in Israel or Jordan, claims

100 different species of coral and 800 species of fish in a stupefying array of colors. Since the water is always 70 to 75 degrees Fahrenheit, the fish and snorkelers have a stable environment in which to swim. I couldn't resist the aqua water for more than a few minutes at a time.

My other weekend adventure beside nature trips was to visit kibbutzim. On a kibbutz halfway between Jerusalem and Tel Aviv, I made friends with Americans and Canadians who founded the kibbutz. Initially, walking into the residential area made up of identical bungalows, I was taken aback by the uniformity, but I soon learned that inside each house there was a very individual type family living with its own decor and lifestyle. My kibbutz friends David and Vivian explained.

"Individuality is necessary here," said Vivian.

"Why?" I asked.

David responded, "We are all North Americans in our thirties and forties. We would never accept the old kibbutz pioneer way of doing things."

I discovered kibbutzim vary tremendously. Some

are religious, some, secular; some are agricultural, some, industrial; some are committed to simplicity, some seek comfortable lifestyles. The kibbutz where I hung out was modern rather than traditional, busily acquiring individual household conveniences like washing machines and microwaves. Except for kibbutz meetings, most people ate their meals at home rather than in the communal dining room. I understood the urge for modern goods and a nuclear family lifestyle, but, as someone who'd absorbed the stories of the early pioneers, I felt regret that collective sharing and responsibility were becoming less the norm.

Could I have lived on a kibbutz, I asked myself. Certainly, early pioneer life would have been too strenuous for my taste but I wondered about today. Kibbutzim appealed to my belief in community solidarity and cooperation, but the lack of freedom would have been impossible for me, especially losing the ability to travel whenever I felt the urge.

The longer I lived in Jerusalem, the more I met people engaged in causes and seeking change in Israeli life. Peace with the Arabs was the overriding issue and my friends – lawyers, doctors, journalists – worked on everything from human rights for Palestinians to defending Israeli soldiers who didn't believe in military service on the West Bank. The peaceniks, many of whom were members of Peace Now, tended to come from university or professional life and were typically Ashkenazim from European family backgrounds. They thought very differently from growing numbers of Israelis, Sephardim, who had been expelled from their homes in Middle Eastern countries and had little faith in peace.

While Israel promoted itself as a home for all Jews, it was obvious that Jews from different ethnic backgrounds rarely mixed and certainly split over the major political issues of the day, whether peace, religion, or allocations in the national budget. I was in Israel the year after the 1982 war in Lebanon when Defense Minister Arik Sharon invaded Lebanon as a way to destroy the PLO and supported attacks by Christian Lebanese on the Sabra and Shatila refugee camps. My Israeli circle of friends had all actively opposed the war and Sharon. They believed negotiation with the PLO was the only possible course of action and were vindicated 25 years later when the government of Israel finally began communicating and negotiating with the Palestinian National Council in the West Bank.

Through my university work, I also came into contact with leaders of the Israeli feminist community which overlapped considerably with that of the peaceniks. While active on issues of sex discrimination and human rights, the feminists also sought to establish connections and hold joint demonstrations with Palestinian women as a way to a peace agreement. I was inspired by the efforts of women on both sides to cross internal boundaries and tried eagerly to get to know some Palestinian women leaders, usually Christians, from nearby Bethlehem.

I came up with the idea of throwing a party for both Israeli and Palestinian women I knew in order to introduce them to each other. My Israeli university friends warned me such a party would be a disaster – political contacts were fine, but socializing, impossible. I didn't listen. I made sure all my guests received a glass of arak (a Middle Eastern alcoholic beverage) as they came in the front door to loosen them up. The party, which started out stiffly, soon mellowed with conversation flowing about jobs and family, but not politics. By the end of the evening the women were exchanging business cards. Unfortunately, few contacts between my guests were ever made. The Palestinian-Israeli divide was too wide to be bridged through socializing.

When I left Israel after six full months, I had gotten deeply enough into Israeli life to feel I was beginning to know it. There was so much that attracted me – the mix of Jews from all over the world, the progressive politics of my peacenik and feminist friends, the extraordinary land from desert to sea. At the same time, I was exhausted. Israel felt like an exceedingly tense country with incessant internal political discussions or arguments and constant anxiety over what its neighbors were up to. Israelis often "relaxed" by leaving home and traveling overseas. I too left Israel feeling it was time for a long rest at my home in the U.S.

Then I got back to California and found my life there lacking. Every day was pleasant, mellow – and lacking in intensity! I missed the fervor of Israel and soon began scheming for a second leave of absence. I applied for a research leave this time and was thrilled when San Jose State, somewhat reluctantly, given my previous year's absence, agreed. Where to go? I had heard the rhyming Israeli expression that translates to "Haifa works, Jerusalem studies, and Tel Aviv dances." Instead of staying again in Jerusalem, I decided to try dancing in Tel Aviv.

The following January, in 1984, I became a Tel Avivi. Through friends, I found a room to rent in an apartment that was a couple of blocks from the beach. Tel Aviv feels like a true seaside town, warm and humid, dotted with outdoor cafes, the beach and sea beckoning at all times. Much of Tel Aviv stays open on Shabbat. It was a place that invited dancing and, unlike the heavy religious atmosphere of Jerusalem, brought out my Mediterranean spirit.

My research work was on the status of women in Israel, which required background reading and then interviews with women leaders in government, the professions, military, and women's service organizations. I was fortunate to be loaned a small office at Tel Aviv University where I did my reading and worked out my interview schedule. My best interview was with a woman army colonel who -- off the record -- detailed examples of sex discrimination in the military.

My daily schedule consisted of research at the university or interviews around town in the morning. I was usually at home by lunchtime for a sandwich in the sun on the roof of my building, then a long walk on the beach or a swim. Evenings were spent cooking with my younger roommates, who were either university students or holding their first jobs. After dinner, we often went out to a café for coffee and ended up chatting with whomever stopped by for conversation. I was even able to do that on Shabbat.

Early in the spring I met up in Eilat with Arnie, an American colleague and old friend, who was on sabbatical in Jerusalem. We crossed the Israeli border to go to Nuweiba, the first major town in the Sinai, which at that time was under Israeli control. In Nuweiba everything was far more exotic than in Eilat. Camels from nearby Bedouin camps lounged around waiting to give visitors rides. I spent most of each day snorkeling in a sea whose color could only be matched by turquoise stone. Right off shore there was a coral wall – fiery red, royal purple, electric green corals with fish shooting by in incandescent zigzags. Our hotel was on a palm-fringed beach with cream-colored, powder-like sand. Every day my friend and I had a lunch of jumbo shrimp grilled with coriander washed down by Omar Khayyam white wine.

When Arnie went back to work in Jerusalem, I stayed in Nuweiba a few extra days and became friendly with Julian, a British staff member at the hotel, who ran a parasailing operation and was known as Abdul Parachute. He invited me to make an excursion to Mount Sinai, and I immediately accepted. We set out in a jeep with a driver at five p.m. in order to catch the desert scenery before the sun set. Hawks careened along the walls of the canyons, flashes of black against pink, beige and mauve layers of rock. We camped near Mount Sinai, or Jebel Musa, as the Muslims call it. Lying in my sleeping bag under a midnight blue sky speckled with thousands of stars, I understood why all the world's great religions claimed the region for their own sacred stories.

At three in the morning, Julian and I were woken by the driver who gave us tea. A half hour later, we began climbing up the mountain's nearly four thousand stone steps that penitent monks had carved fifteen hundred years earlier. The climb was surprisingly easy because the air was cool and we rested a lot. After a couple of hours, we put away our flashlights and watched the ridges turn a delicate pink. Soon pale gold light made the mountains a patchwork of ochre, burnt umber, terra cotta, carnelian.

We sat, about 750 steps from the summit, in a natural amphitheater where tradition holds that the seventy elders of Israel waited while Moses spoke with God. I felt I was living the Bible.

At the summit, we sat on a rock ledge as shooting rays of sun illuminated ridge after mountainous ridge, making the stones somehow resemble waves on the ocean. The sight was etched in my heart, something I would always remember. After a while Julian and I greeted an Arab family sitting nearby and they offered us dates. As we rested – a Jewish woman, a Christian man, and Arab parents with their young son – I said a silent prayer that our three traditions could, in the same way, come together in harmony.

When I returned to Tel Aviv from the Sinai, I attended a Purim party to celebrate a holiday based on the story of Esther and, like Hallowe'en, a costume party. I decked myself out in a Kenyan costume and, in a crazy mood, darkened my face with shoe polish. When I took off my headpiece, Avital, the man I was dancing with, who certainly knew I was not African, was nonetheless shocked to see blond hair. An eventful beginning to an eventful relationship. I was strongly attracted to Avital and began spending my weekends with him at his old Arab house in the German Colony of Jerusalem.

I rather liked being a commuter between Tel Aviv and Jerusalem since the two cities were so different. Also, being in Jerusalem gave me a chance to see more of my friend Daphna, a translator from German or English to Hebrew, who lived around the corner and visited with me or met me for coffee most days that I was there. I should, however, have listened to Daphna's warnings about Avital. I thoroughly enjoyed his cultural awareness and meeting his friends from the performing arts world. There were also low points when, certain I couldn't understand much Hebrew, Avital spoke on the phone and made dates with other women. I didn't expect monogamy, but I did expect discretion.

Back in Tel Aviv, I came to the end of my research on the status of women in Israel. While Israel articulated an ideology of sexual equality, reality did not come at all close. The army, supposedly a bastion of equal status, reinforced discrimination by giving men potentially heroic combat roles and assigning women to clerical or training jobs. In civilian life, women were oppressed by the primacy of their family roles as mother, child-rearer and homemaker, which resulted in their working mainly as part-timers who earned far less than men. Public policy reinforced the primacy of women's family roles and the secondary status of their work roles. Despite the demands of a small women's movement, I doubted women's status would undergo much change in the foreseeable future. When I finished writing, I titled my monograph, "In the Land of the Patriachs: Public Policy on Women in Israel." I suspect patriarchal society, pun aside, remains an apt description.

As I was concluding my leave of absence, I became friendly with the Greek Consul in Jerusalem, who helped me make arrangements for my upcoming summer program in Greece. Over lunches, he told me about his job as a diplomat. He had many contacts in the Palestinian Occupied Territories and seemed to know as much about developments there as any Israelis I knew. Diplomacy sounded like a compelling career, although I knew little about it.

I investigated the process for becoming a U.S. diplomat, becoming acquainted with some Americans at the U.S. Embassy in Tel Aviv and the U.S. Consulate in Jerusalem. The more I learned, the more intrigued I became. Then I found out about a special admissions program in the State Department for women and minorities. If accepted, I could make a lateral career entry and start my diplomatic career in a mid-level post. I applied.

My two leaves of absence in Israel gave me a strong appetite for living overseas. I loved getting to know a country in greater depth and being challenged to adapt to a new lifestyle. As it turned out, my whim of applying to the State Department soon evolved into a possible career when I was admitted to the Foreign Service. I decided to leave my home in California and switch from academia to diplomacy. A restless creature, I was ready for something new and for greatly expanded opportunities I would have... to travel.

When I left Israel the second time, I no longer felt the ambivalence I had experienced earlier. While I was still enraptured by Israel's natural features and had many dear Israeli friends, the intensity of life was, finally, too extreme for me. I would never have given up my two years in Israel, however. In those years, I not only reached out to a whole new world of Middle Eastern culture, but I also internalized Jewish history in a way that comes from living in the "homeland." As much as I disagreed with right wing Israeli politics and strongly resisted the merging of religion and civil society, I grew and deepened as a woman who was born Jewish but had matured without much religious identity. In a strange and unexpected way, the words of the professor on my first flight to Israel became imbued with special meaning. *Ilana, welcome home.*

Baltic Roots

While many Europeans have ventured off to Estonia, Latvia and Lithuania, those countries remain a mystery to most Americans. What a shame. I have traveled three times to the Baltics, where I enjoyed the wonders of Europe for half the price and launched a search for my "roots" in Latvia and Lithuania, the lands of my forebears.

I didn't choose Estonia as my first Baltic destination. It chose me.

In 1995 Jim and I were in Greece for the summer and decided to go to Russia on our <u>free</u> Delta Airlines tickets which we'd received by happily agreeing to be bumped from a transatlantic flight. Jim had served in the

US Embassy in Moscow in the 1970s when Russia was still very much the Soviet Union. By 1995, it was Russia again, a place I'd never been. For me, the extra of this trip would be a side excursion to Riga, Latvia.

Before leaving Athens, I checked with the Latvian Embassy and was told that, with American passports, we could purchase our visas upon arrival. So we reserved a sleeper on an overnight train from St. Petersburg to Riga, stocked up on vodka and orange juice, and, imbibing screwdrivers, played Scrabble until we were sleepy enough to curl up, womb-like, in our pint-sized berths.

The train stopped at the Latvian-Russian border at six in the morning, and the Russian border guards gruffly checked for escapees or contraband, presumably stored under the cramped seats. Next on board were the Latvian border police checking passports and visas. Of course, we had no visas. Fortunately, Jim could explain in Russian that we'd been told we could get visas upon arrival. "At the airport," a young man barked, "not here." Armed with a rifle, he ordered us to close up our suitcases and follow him. He kept our passports.

We barely had time to throw on our jeans. On the platform another policeman grabbed our bags and we anxiously followed him down a path to a wooden building surrounded by thick forest, literally in the middle of nowhere. We were instructed to sit on a bench in a bare room while another rifle-laden policeman guarded us. To add to my anxiety, all the policemen looked like teenagers, capable of shooting but not necessarily able to handle distraught foreigners.

When our train pulled out without us, I went into panic mode. I had Holocaust visions, picturing executions in the forest around us where, in fact, many executions of Jews and Communists took place during World War II. I urged Jim to tell the guard we wanted to call the American Embassy in Riga. Jim communicated in Russian. The guard looked at us with contempt then shook his head. Jim finally determined from him that the building had no phone. The guard informed us the boss was sending our passport numbers by radio to Riga for clearance.

We sat, essentially imprisoned, for an hour. I kept shivering, chills along my spine. Finally, the boss, a young man of perhaps twenty, came in and handed us our passports. He grumbled that we would be leaving on the next train.

"To Riga?" I squeaked.

"*Nyet*," he growled.

"To St. Petersburg?"

"*Nyet*," again.

"Then, where?" I moaned.

The boss muttered, "To Tallinn. Estonia."

I had only a vague idea where Estonia was, but I was willing to go anywhere to escape the border police. Tallinn sounded just fine. When we climbed onto the train, I was deliriously happy to be free and see Western Europeans in the car. We collapsed on a seat behind an Irish couple and told them our story. Sympathetic, they handed us their tour book on Estonia. I searched for a luxury hotel, not my usual preference, but I wanted to recover in luxury from the morning's stress. I chose the four-star Olympia because it had a Greek name that beckoned me

The hotel was a tall tower, new and well-appointed with a view across the Baltic Sea to Helsinki. After our trauma at the Latvian border, I collapsed on the bed, sipped coffee, watched CNN, and soaked up a sense of security and well-being. After a long hot bath, I was finally ready to brave the real world. Using a hotel map, Jim and I walked to Old Town, a superb medieval community behind centuries-old walls. It contained dignified Protestant churches, tall and narrow pastel-colored buildings, and cobbled streets winding through town to the square. We climbed church spires for views of Old Town, wandered into numerous antique shops selling 19th century spinning wheels and wooden cookware, and ate ice cream at one of the many outdoor cafes on the square.

In the history museum, I began learning about Baltic resistance to the Soviets whose occupation began in World War II, and Estonia's joyful return to independence in 1990. While many Russians continue to live in the Baltics, they are, understandably, not well-received. Likewise, ugly Soviet-style, cube-like apartment buildings and industries stand in stark contrast to Baltic homes with carved, colorfully painted wood and flower boxes. The people of the Baltics adore nature and, when dressed in native costumes, they seem to explode in color with embroidery in red, yellow and blue.

Two aspects of Estonia puzzled me. First, Estonian is a Finno-Ugric language, related to Finnish and Hungarian, which looks and sounds like nothing I have ever known. As just one example, "good morning" is "tere ommikust." I could find no cognates to languages I spoke and was completely disconcerted when I tried to decipher street names or store signs. Fortunately, most Estonians speak some, or very good, English.

Then, there's the Estonian character. Upon arrival, I picked up a small guidebook in the hotel lobby which informed me in its first sentence that Estonians rarely smile. I didn't believe a word of it until I tried joking with hotel or restaurant staff. No response except a respectful nod of the head. Since I was in mood of celebration, I longed for a warmer connection. Later, when I heard laughter in the streets, I rushed close, seeking a droll Estonian only to discover the merrymakers were Russian tourists. While I'm sure Estonians experience moments of happiness, I wasn't in Tallinn long enough to figure out how they express warmth and pleasure.

On our fifth and last day in Tallinn, we caught the train back to St. Petersburg, and from there, flew back to Greece. While I enjoyed Tallinn, I didn't rush back to the Baltic States, perhaps due to my experience on the Russian-Latvian border. It took another nine years before I again set out for the Baltics. My interest revived in 2003 when, working in Washington, D.C., I got to know the director of the US-Baltic Society whose office was down the hall from mine. When he discovered my heritage, he loaned me material on Latvia and Lithuania and offered to get me relatively inexpensive airplane tickets to those countries.

While I had never previously been interested in my roots, I began researching historical archives to see if I might be able to find out about my grandparents and great-grandparents. Both sides of my immediate family had emigrated from Eastern Europe to the U.S. in the late nineteenth century and, like so many immigrants, had thrown themselves into Americanization. I never asked my grandparents before they died about their lives in the home country, something I came to regret. By the time I reached middle age, perhaps related to my own aging, I wanted to know where the seeds of my life were sown and what struggles had brought us to America. Moreover, family research would require travel, an always welcome excuse to set off for someplace new.

My problem in tracing my own genealogy was that I had no records and little family information. To make matters worse, I read that records in the Baltics were haphazard at best since the lands in the nineteenth century kept falling under different occupiers – Poland, Russia, and Germany. For my Latvian maternal grandfather, I found through Ellis Island records a ship passenger list indicating that he, a five year old, had arrived in New York with his parents in 1892, on a ship from Hamburg called *Columbia*. I also knew he had lived in Liepaya, Latvia (Libau in Yiddish), but I had no address or other information.

When Jim and I arrived in Riga, we spent a few days sightseeing, visiting neighborhoods with stunning Art Nouveau architecture, much of it designed by Mikhail Eisenstein, the father of Sergei Eisenstein, the Russian film-maker. I loved the curves and fancy iron work, the stained glass and sculptures that adorn Art Nouveau buildings, and Riga had some of the best in Europe.

When we eventually found the state archives, we were told by an officious woman bureaucrat that it would take six months to do a search based on my grandfather's name. Fortunately, Jim, speaking Russian, mentioned that the family was Jewish and we were directly referred to the young woman who specialized in Jewish genealogy. In a half hour of searching the records of Leipaja, my grandfather's home town, she found a birth certificate for one of my grandfather's brothers. I was ecstatic – we'd found actual proof of the family. The archivist then told me my great grandfather's occupation was listed on the certificate as shoemaker. That small detail thrilled me. Suddenly my forebears were flesh and blood, hardworking people who hammered nails into leather.

I persuaded Jim to visit Liepaja and we took a bus through the rolling Latvian countryside of fields and forests to the Baltic coast. Our hotel staff informed me the Jewish quarter of Leipaja had run several blocks along the park in front of the sand dunes. Jim and I wandered the area with nothing to orient us except an odd feeling that one of the charming but decaying wooden cottages might have been my family's home. When we crossed the dunes to the beach and I stared at the blue-gray Baltic, I got an eerie sense that my family's proximity to the sea explained my passion for it.

Back in Riga, we visited the impressive Jewish Museum to learn more of the history of the Jews in

Latvia. The Jews of Liepaja were killed by the Nazis and their Latvian collaborators in several massacres at the beginning of World War II. The last remaining portion of the community was slaughtered in the dunes in December, 1941. I will never forget a shocking photograph of naked Jewish women, backs to the camera, standing on the dunes holding their babies above their heads before they were shot down. While, by then, my own family was safe in America, I felt strangely connected to those women in the dunes and ached for their cruel demise.

Our next stop was the lovely town of Vilnius, Lithuania's capital. The old city was huge and full of monuments, boutiques, restaurants and cafes. Lithuania is predominantly Catholic and grand churches graced the streets to the main square. There were also many vendors with booths on the streets, selling amber from the Baltic Sea and carved wooden crafts. I couldn't resist several pairs of amber earrings. I learned to test the validity of a piece of amber by holding a lighted match next to it – plastic will melt, amber won't.

On the back streets of the old city, I discovered jazz clubs and neighborhood restaurants. The back streets also showed the way the actual residents live as compared to the chic and sophisticated tourist buildings around the square. The residents' homes were simple and dated, although the owners were slowly acquiring home appliances and heating systems. The exteriors of the houses appeared attractive, again with bright paint and window boxes full of flowers

Now, for my "roots" experience. Lithuania was less personally compelling than Latvia because I had even less information about my paternal grandfather. Jim and I again went to the national archives to try to learn about people named Ben Porat, my original family name. From a cousin's research I knew my great-grandfather and his wife had arrived at Ellis Island in 1887, but from where? Ellis Island had no records. We also knew my great uncle had lived in Grodno, once part of the Lithuanian principality, but, by the nineteenth century, Grodno was under the Russian Empire. Were my roots there?

Fortunately, Jim, who loved combing the Web, had an interest in genealogy. We had a bit of information from his research. He discovered a figure, Menashe Ben Porat, whose name was the same as my original name. Ben Porat was a well-known Jewish judge (*dayan*) who died in 1831 in Smorgon, a small town in Lithuania. If I had my druthers, I'd like to be descended from a famous jurist, but I had nothing to actually link me to him. Unfortunately, the Vilnius archivist was unable to help, especially since the first Russian census took place some years after my great grandfather had already emigrated.

Despite my inability to find my own Lithuanian connections, I was deeply moved by the history of the Jews of Lithuania, a much larger and more prominent community than in Latvia and well documented in the Jewish Museum in Vilnius. Outstanding Jewish scholars and leaders thrived in the nineteenth century and earlier, but the entire Jewish community was lost in the Holocaust.

I was touched by our museum guide, a young, non-Jewish university student who volunteered in the museum as community service.

The Baltics have worked hard to make amends to Jews for the devastation of World War II. Jewish museums have made it possible for descendants to learn about their forebears' communities even if they don't find actual family records. I was struck by the words of Latvian President Vike-Freiberga who spoke before the World Congress of Jews of Latvian Descent in 2001: *Latvia is also your home, home of the Latvian Jews. Whether it is your fatherland, or the land of your family's roots, Latvia is also your land, it is part of your experience, and your ancestors have contributed to it.* If the Baltics were willing to reach out to their Jewish descendants, I was more than ready to reclaim my Baltic heritage.

At the same time, I was also fascinated by Lithuania's old, pre-Christian religion. The only Lithuanian I knew of before my journey to Vilnius was Marija Gimbutas, a multifaceted scholar who combined anthropology, mythology, linguistics, ethnology and archeology. She spent much of her career at Harvard and UCLA, where she produced tomes on Neolithic and Bronze Age cultures in what she called "Old Europe," Central and Southeastern Europe. Her revolutionary findings pointed to Neolithic goddess-centered and woman-centered civilization that was destroyed by patriarchal invaders in the Bronze Age. While Gimbutas' thinking is challenged by some, her research has been embraced by many, including the feminist movement, as validation of ancient women-centered societies. Her work spoke to my desire to honor female power from the past and reconstitute it today.

Gimbutas also immersed herself in Lithuanian folklore and wrote extensively about pre-Christian religion in the Baltics. Medieval Lithuanian religion, known as Romuva, was practiced for centuries but suppressed during the Soviet Occupation. In 1992, it was again recognized as a Baltic faith, and today followers practice ancient customs and celebrate ancient rituals. I was eager to meet the people who kept old Baltic traditions alive.

I was honored to be invited to the home of Jonas and Iniya Trinkunas, who are the Prince and Princess of Romuva religion today. The polytheistic religion is grounded in ancient mythology and nature. It celebrates with seasonal outdoor ceremonies, feasts of traditional food, and dance and rituals in old world costume. The Trinkunas couple showed me videos of their large summer Solstice festival which coincides with the national festival of St. Jonas (St. John's day in much of Europe). They told me about their followers, holidays, community feasts and traditions, and shared CDs of old music recorded by their choirs. The Trinkunas family has worked hard to spread knowledge about Old Lithuanian religion around the world and have joined with other neo-pagan groups. After meeting the Trinkunas family, I felt a strong urge to return to the Baltics sometime to participate in a neo-pagan celebration.

Sometime came the next year when I led a group of women to Latvia and Lithuania in 2005. To get to know Baltic women we held meetings with women leaders in government organizations, including visiting delightful President Vike Freiberga of Latvia in her palace. We also met activists in a wide range of NGOs providing women's services and working on anti-discrimination law. My group was surprised to discover that, post-Communism, women were facing a harder time finding jobs than in the Soviet period when women's employment was a given.

Sadly, the one new area of employment for women was sex tourism. Social openness and a lack of jobs for women was drawing rural women to cities where they ended up working in bars or in organized prostitution. While sex tourism was rationalized by some as providing incomes for low income or unemployed women, we learned that professional sex workers were in competition with young girls from the countryside who, attracted by the idea of meeting foreigners, often offered themselves for free. British stag parties, using cheap charter flights and package deals, produced the rowdiest offenders in Riga, with gangs of drunkens roaming the streets into the wee hours. Neither municipal officials nor business people realized that uncontrolled sex tourism would ultimately drive away other tourists, as well as lead to an increase in AIDS and trafficking. Apparently, in 2009, the Riga municipal government finally caught on and established an evening tourist police force to tamp down drunken behavior.

Happily, my women's group eventually got to take part in some Baltic pagan rituals. In Riga, we were invited by followers of the Dievturi religion to an evening gathering. We congregated in a backyard, stood in a circle around a large oak tree, held candles against the dark blue sky, and listened to the group's old songs and prayers to ancient gods and goddesses. After the ritual, we sipped wine and spoke with the few group members who knew English. They were eager for us to let the world know their ancient beliefs are alive and well.

In Vilnius, we celebrated Saint Jonas' Festival on June 24th, a big holiday across Lithuania. While most European countries celebrate midsummer day in some way, Lithuanians had a particularly lively agenda. Wearing wreaths of wild flowers and traditional costumes, they went to the countryside or to city parks to picnic, sing and dance until the sun set which was late at night in this northern clime. Traditions, all derived from pagan beliefs, included searching for the magic fern blossom at midnight, jumping over bonfires (as in Greece), greeting the rising midsummer sun, washing the face with morning dew, and floating flowers on the waters of a river or lake.

Perhaps because I had relished tracing my own Jewish roots, I could feel in my bones the significance to the Baltic peoples of keeping their own roots alive. From family names to silver pieces of jewelry in ancient designs to singing (which Baltic peoples took such pride in), the Baltics, no longer occupied by their neighbors, vigorously maintained their ancient identity as a way of owning their place in history. I felt proud to have Baltic roots. Mine were Jewish, but in some profound way, also pagan. I could rejoice in the mother goddess just as I could feel the pain of Baltic Jews suffering oppression. Inspired by goddess-centered Old Europe and Jewish survival, it was easy to claim my place in the Baltic world.

PART III

WOMEN HOLD UP MORE THAN HALF THE SKY

Indigenous Women Down Under

"Women hold up half the sky." This Chinese saying suggests women play equal roles with men in society. In truth, women hold up much more than half, especially in developing countries where they do three-quarters of the work and, almost alone, care for families. From 2003 to 2009, I traveled with women's groups or my family to countries I barely knew in order to learn, from face to face encounters, about indigenous women and women in Asia.

Telling the stories of women is often heart-wrenching. I remember talking with a Nepalese woman who walked, bleeding from her uterus, on treacherous mountain trails for three days to get medical treatment after she was attacked by her husband. I recall hearing an Aboriginal woman in Australia, one of the Stolen Generation, describe being taken from her mother at age five and sent to live with a white family where she ended up working as a servant and being raped by the "man" of the house. In Guatemala, a Mayan woman told me about being imprisoned for months in a pit underground because military forces believed they could make her expose guerilla fighters in her family.

There are millions such stories, even though women's status has improved marginally in recent years. These stories make me angry and sad. I cannot visit beautiful locations without also discovering how women struggle in those places and how non-governmental organizations seek to empower women in the development process. I start Part III with Australia, a developed country with a small and troubled indigenous community.

Strange circumstances brought me to Australia in 2003.

Jim and I had moved to California and were happily hosting our Greek god-daughter while she attended Santa Rosa Junior College. In 2002, I was selected for a Fulbright Fellowship, a U.S. government award given to American academics. My assignment was to teach and do research at a university in Surabaya, Indonesia, an exotic country with hundreds of islands, a gentle form of Islam, fabulous arts, and Southeast Asian food. Then, in October, 2002, terrorist bombs exploded in a tourist district on the island paradise of Bali, Indonesia, killing hundreds, mostly foreigners. The world was shocked. As a precaution the U.S. Consulate in Surabaya sent all non-essential American personnel back to the United States.

Anxious about attacks on foreigners, I requested an assignment elsewhere. After much delay, I was told I could be reassigned anywhere in the Asia region as long as I worked out the arrangements on my own. They gave me three weeks to do so. I sent out several emails to foreign universities, saying, essentially, "Fully funded Fulbrighter with nowhere to go." I was extremely fortunate that the University of Sydney invited me to give a series of lectures on women and development and do research on a topic of my choice.

I set off in January, 2003, with Jim and our Greek god-daughter Katerina for a semester of Australian life. As a late arrival to the Australian program, I had to get settled without help from either Fulbright or the university. I thought it would be easy to find housing, but I was completely wrong. In Sydney's nicer neighborhoods short-term rentals were extremely expensive and required year-long leases. Anything short-term and affordable on my housing allowance, such as a foreign student rental, was ugly and dirty.

After three jetlagged days of searching, we heard about a rental in Darling Harbor that was just barely affordable. Desperate, on the verge of renting without even seeing the place, we met the agent for a viewing just before another interested client. Taken by the attractive, modern building and neighborhood, I signed a lease the moment we walked in the door of the flat. Darling Harbor was a delightful inlet, surrounded by outdoor cafes where customers consumed gigantic glasses of beer, ethnic restaurants reeking of garlic, and elegant tourist shops. Katerina and I often strolled around Darling Harbor, sometimes encountering costumed street actors parading around on stilts or posing statue-like in gold or silver as historical figures or celebrities.

It was fateful we ended up a block from the harbor since, as a lover of all bodies of water, Sydney Harbor became the reason I embraced the city. There is no way to appreciate the size of Sydney Harbor from looking at a map or crossing one of the bridges. It is just too large, with a curvy perimeter of almost 200 miles. We explored the harbor through "walkabout," the Australian phrase for making a ramble somewhere. Jim, Katerina and I would take the Metro down to Circular Quay, across from the Opera House, where there is a line-up of municipal ferries that cross to distant shores. We either chugged off to a planned destination or hopped on the first departing boat to ramble wherever it took us.

We often escaped the urban environment by sailing to Watson's Bay, a waterfront town on the south shore with bayside fish restaurants and cottage homes surrounded by gardens and wild flowers. A short walk took us to South Point where we had the bay on one side and the crashing ocean on the other. On the way to South Point was a beach called Lady Bay. At this nude beach, the water is unbelievably clean, as it is all around the bay. I was immediately ready to shed my clothes. Jim and Katerina were unwilling to disrobe but willing to watch. It was great fun to join other naked sunbathers and swim out to a boat offshore that sold ice cream popsicles, then paddle back to shore with three ice creams in a hand above my head.

In contrast, for hearty swimmers, there were ocean beaches, reached by ferry or bus, that made Sydney's suburbs a surfer's, although not a swimmer's, paradise. Considering myself a strong swimmer, I eagerly dove into the surf at Bondi Beach, was pummeled by a wave, thrown forward, and turned over and over until I hit the sand with my entire body. Finally, tossed onto the shore, I could barely get to my feet. I understood why the beaches were lined by lifeguards who, looking charming in their round red swim caps, were sorely needed by swimmers like me. From then on, I chose to bathe in scenic swimming holes of salt water nestled in rocky cliffs above the ocean.

Lest it seem that Sydney was all play, I should describe my life at Sydney University. The campus, containing a beautiful quad with an emerald lawn and an impressive set of sandstone buildings in the style of "Victorian Academic Gothic," made me feel as if I were in England. Unfortunately, inside, I found only typical theater-like lecture halls, seminar rooms, and offices. When I gave formal lectures in the large halls facing a hundred or more students, I had no opportunity to chat with students one on one. When I taught seminar classes, I did get to know the students a bit, but they seemed to feel somewhat constrained, unfamiliar with free-wheeling American style of give-and-take.

I had a better experience doing research. I chose the topic of gun control, one of my strong interests in the U.S. and an area in which Australia had made remarkable strides. I found a faculty colleague who was an expert on gun laws and who helped me find the documentary and scholarly materials I needed. He also suggested I interview a number of government experts and some leading members of Parliament. I was sure it would be difficult to get to these officials, but they were remarkably willing to meet, perhaps because a visiting Fulbright scholar gave me a certain cachet.

I ended up producing a study on the impact of Australia's new gun laws on homicide and suicide, which I presented at the university. Australia was proud of its restrictive laws and relieved to know they were having a positive impact. Someone from the university newspaper wrote a piece about my research that led to a full-page article in the <u>Sydney Morning Herald</u>. I was stunned to receive so much notice since in the U.S. gun control desperately struggles for media attention. It helped to be an admiring foreigner.

Sydney also presented a long-awaited opportunity to learn about Aborigines, Australia's extraordinary indigenous people who have survived 50,000 years but today are only three percent of the population. When I arrived at Sydney "Uni," I sought out courses in Indigenous Studies, but, to my amazement, no one in my department knew the location of the Indigenous Studies Department. Several faculty warned me that Aboriginal faculty members lacked Ph.D.s and were therefore "less than scholarly," to my ears, a comment tinged with racism. Fortunately, I paid no heed and sat in on an introductory course that was lively and compelling.

Soon after our arrival in Sydney, some Aboriginal leaders were meeting to organize that year's "Sorry Day." The annual event commemorated the government's removal in the late 19th and early 20th centuries of Aboriginal children from their families in order to have them raised for their "betterment" in white homes or orphanages. Often these children were neglected and even abused. By 2003, they had matured to the age of senior citizens and were known as the "Stolen Generation." Aborigines were demanding a government apology.

At the time we arrived in Sydney, the Australian government had been dominated for years by conservatives who refused to apologize. At the Sorry Day meeting at the Opera House, Jim, Katerina and I attended an open gathering of Aboriginal leaders. Newcomers to Australia, we were struck by the Aborigines' reasonable-sounding demands and the stubborn refusal of the government to acknowledge past injustices, not unlike the U.S. government's dealings with Native Americans, African Americans and interned Japanese citizens during World War II. The ongoing clash between Aborigines and whites surfaced many times during our stay. While we occasionally met whites genuinely concerned about Aborigines, we also encountered many educated people, including supposed liberals, who had written them off as drunken, lazy and spoiled by government welfare programs, terms that would not be tolerated in American public discourse.

To enlighten Katerina about Aborigines, we often turned to Australian films which featured Aborigines resisting exploitation in the Outback or struggling to adapt to urban life, stark contrasts to popular images of Aborigines as derelicts. We visited the Australian Museum which had an informative Indigenous Australians exhibit that taught the prehistory and life patterns of Aborigines. The presentation emphasized that, going back 50,000 years, Aborigines found ways to live in the barren and challenging environment of the Outback where few non-indigenous people have any idea how to live off the land.

I was also captured by Aboriginal and Torres Islander art on display at the Art Gallery of New South Wales. I had seen a few pieces of Aboriginal art previously, but viewing artists from all over the country, working in their particular styles and utilizing available regional materials, was breathtaking. Some Aboriginal art parallels modern art with abstract patterns, blocks of earthy colors, and innovative techniques such as dot painting and sand painting. While the art appears abstract, it expresses tribal tradition and myth, conveying "Dreamtime" associations with land and ancestors. Once viewers understand Aboriginal iconography, they can witness the intense connection of Aborigines to their territory. Today fine Aboriginal painting has become a genre sought by collectors around the world and Aborigine artists are considered creative geniuses.

Between the miracle of Aboriginal survival and the skill of Aboriginal artists, Australia's indigenous peoples earned my deep respect. Of course, I knew many Aborigines in the Outback, brutalized by European occupation and self-destructive through use of alcohol and drugs, lived marginal lives. Yet, many Aborigines had also become successful urban dwellers, thriving professionals and business people, which made white Australian stereotypes seem even more ignorant and oppressive.

On a second trip to Australia two years later, I brought a group of American women for a women's studies institute. We started with workshops at Sydney "Uni," then traveled to South Australia, where we visited an area called the Coorong near the mouth of the Murray River. There we met up with some of the Ngarrindjeri people who have established a cultural center and wilderness lodge as a way to teach non-Aboriginals "our traditions and relationships to the land, water, trees, plants and animals." The cultural center provided a glimpse of Ngarrindjeri life – customs, dreaming stories, baskets woven from river reeds. Camp Coorong offered rooms, meals and bushwalks around the marshes and lagoons to demonstrate how local people lived with nature.

Our women's group was eager to get to know Ngarrindjeri women, whose story about the threat to their sacred site on Hindmarsh Island at the river's mouth was known across Australia. Aboriginal women enact their sacred practices separately from their male community;

their "sacred business" is kept secret from all outsiders. When real estate developers announced a plan to build a bridge to Hindmarsh Island and construct homes and a yacht harbor on their sacred grounds, Ngarrindjeri women appealed to government agencies. A Royal Commission investigated. Unfortunately, a breach surfaced among the Aboriginal women with some calling the claim to sacred land a fabrication. The confusion intensified when the original claimants refused to testify before males and reveal their secrets.

By the time our women's group met with the Ngarrindjeri women, the developers had won and the bridge had been built. The women, refusing to use it, crossed to the island by boat. We met with the women on land under the end of the bridge where the women recounted their tale of exploitation. After they spoke, American and Aboriginal women joined hands in a healing ceremony. The Aboriginal women pleaded for sisterhood across cultures and we felt honored they had reached out to us. One Aboriginal woman sang in a tongue none of the Americans recognized, but her plaintive notes brought tears to our eyes. After we broke the circle, we all hugged and stroked each other's backs. The distance between us had disappeared.

We were never told by the women what their "sacred business" entailed. Many authors have written about Hindmarsh Island and one reported it was a place where Ngarrindjeri women went to abort fetuses resulting from rape by a white male. Whether or not that was the case, I believe Aboriginal women have a right to their own sacred space, especially if that space is sanctified by tradition, myth and ritual. Perhaps the most moving moment in our healing ritual came when an American woman, who was part Cherokee and lived on Cherokee land in Florida, presented wooden boxes made from trees on her own sacred land to her indigenous sisters. Ironically, further development of Hindmarsh island was delayed due to the drying of the river from upstream man-made dams and a resulting change in the water content from fresh to salt water. It seemed a victory for nature and people living close to nature and a defeat for the developers, although the natural river must be restored to its natural flow.

Speaking of nature, no one can write about Australia without mentioning its endemic fauna, although I must confess I was disappointed by my initial encounters. Kangaroos were a lot smaller in reality than in my imagination, often not even six feet tall. I had envisioned them as towering over humans. Still, it was marvelous to see them romping through the wilds! Then, there were Koala bears, those huggable, contemplative souls. They appear charming, but sleep continuously, probably from chewing all those soporific gum tree leaves.

For me, Australia's birds and sea lions provided the most thrilling wildlife experiences. While the kookaburra and the emu are its best known birds, Australia has 800 bird species with perhaps the largest number of endemic birds in the world. When visiting friends at their country home in New South Wales, Jim and I watched rainbow-colored lorakeets and orange-crested cockatiels swoop onto feeders on the veranda for breakfast. Fearless, they also gently swooped onto hands and heads. Despite many riotously colored Australian birds, including huge numbers of wild parrots, I personally fell in love with the gallah and its subdued but gorgeous shades of pink and gray. For visitors who don't get into the countryside, Australian birds are definitely worth seeing in captivity. While, at Sydney's Taronga Zoo, tourists typically head to the mammals or marsupials, the bird cage with its chromatic displays was a breathtaking treat.

During our stay Jim and I made an excursion with friends to Kangaroo Island, south of Adelaide, while Katerina stayed in Sydney to complete university work. Kangaroo Island was large, almost all of it a wildlife sanctuary. We first saw the fairy penguins that nest on Kangaroo Island and are visible only at night when they groom themselves and feed their young. At roughly a foot high and weighing a couple of pounds, they are a miniature delight found only in southern Australia and New Zealand.

Then we were mesmerized by fur seals in the hundreds basking, roaring, gallumping across headlands on the rocky southwestern corner of the island. Knowing the astronomical number of seals killed in the nineteenth century by sailors and trappers from around the world, I can only imagine what the coastline looked like with thousands and thousands of seals on its shores and in its waters. Destroying nature for profit has traditionally been a male occupation although undoubtedly a few women have been caught in the profit machine. Still, through the ages, women have been the growers and preservers, not the hunters. As the Aboriginal women taught me, our goal must be living in nature, not in sealskin coats.

My fears for the preservation of nature were deepened even more by my visit to the Great Barrier Reef. There can't be anything more galvanizing in the world's seas than the reef. Before I went to Australia, I imagined the reef as a convenient offshore location. In fact, it is quite a ways out to sea and, if you are staying on shore, as Jim and I were in Cairns, it can be visited only by taking a two to three hour boat ride out to sea. On a future visit I will stay on one of the reef's islands in order to make snorkeling an easy dive into the water. Still, despite a long boat ride, the marine splendor was beyond anything imaginable. I will never forget a dark indigo brain coral the size of Volkswagen. I came away from the reef praying it will be preserved for all time. Although less than ten percent of the 1000 mile long archipelago is accessible to tourists, I fear this massive natural wonder, visible from space, is becoming a victim of humankind through pollution and global warming.

From what I saw of Australia, I felt both at home (Australia's cities have adopted many American cultural characteristics) and filled with wanderlust to see more of the wild and diverse parts of the continent. I felt at the end of my first long stay that I would have been happy being born Australian. For one thing, the country has the right physical dimensions – endless amounts of territory and not very many people (at approximately 22 million, just over half the population of California). A small population makes it easier to accomplish change, and that appeals to me. At the same time, a continent of varied and relatively undeveloped terrain provides a plethora of travel adventures without ever having to use a passport. And when Australians do feel the urge to go overseas, they have Southeast Asia, China, and the Pacific within easy range.

When I told friends in the U.S. about my interest in living in Australia, I always got the same reaction: "It's so far away." When I'd previously expressed my desire to live in Greece, approximately the same number of air miles from California, no one ever objected that Greece was too far away. Why the difference? Partly, cultural familiarity, I think. Westerners are familiar with Greece from studying world history. Hardly anyone ever studies Australia. Also the difference lies in latitude and longitude. Athens is at the same latitude as Washington, D.C., though longitudinally distant. Sydney is roughly the same distance from San Francisco as Athens in flight time, but latitudinally in the Southern Hemisphere and longitudinally across the

International Dateline. When Americans are dreaming of a white Christmas, Australians are at the beach. This makes Australia seem exceptionally far away.

None of those differences phased me. What really made me hesitant about moving was imagining my life in Australia, almost certainly in my beloved harbor city, Sydney. The good news was life would be a lot more peaceful. Australia has much lower crime levels than the U.S., in large part because of strict firearms laws. Then, while Australia plays a role in world affairs, it is much less engaged in world conflict than the U.S. and, for the most part, is happy to be far away from others' conflicts. When I lived in Sydney, I went to anti-war protests to keep Australia out of the American war in Iraq!

The bad news was I couldn't imagine what kind of work I would do in Australia. Of course, I could work on the issues that consume me – women's rights, gun control, human rights for Aborigines – but I would always be an outsider, a foreigner. I'd never be speaking with the credibility of a native. Since progressive politics and community action are such big elements of my life, I couldn't envision living in a place where I might get attention but, because of nationality, my influence would be marginalized.

My consideration of Australian residency taught me a lesson. For me, home is where my politics are, where I can act on social issues in a like-minded, familiar environment. Much as I love being out in the world, much as travel continually lures me away from home, I need to return to a place where I can make a difference.

Guatemala's Indigenous People

In 1980, a university colleague in foggy San Francisco invited me to accompany him for a short visit to Guatemala and I accepted. I was eager to go somewhere, anywhere, with sun. Today, I remember only two parts of our vacation. First, the chicken bus we took from Antigua to Panajachel, a marijuana-smoking hippie haven in the highlands. The vividly painted chicken buses got their name from squawking poultry tied to the roof, being transported to or from local markets. The bus interior wasn't much better than the outside. I recall hard wooden seats, which, due to a lack of shock absorbers, produced bone-crushing jolts as we bounced over potholes in the asphalt or crevasses in dirt roads.

My other memory was my first sight of Lake Atitlan. Standing at the lake's shore, I gazed across at three looming, gray-green volcanoes with wisps of clouds floating between the peaks. The scene felt primeval – and my intoxication was not from a marijuana contact high. Mayan villages dotted the lake's shore, but they were not visible from where I stood. All I saw were dark green forests on steep hillsides, blue-gray water rippling in a steady breeze, volcanoes among the clouds. It felt like a world from a previous millennium. My friend and I had only one day to spend at Lake Atitlan, but I promised myself I would return to one of the most majestic places on earth.

It took me almost thirty years to keep my promise. In both 2008 and 2009, I came back to Guatemala to lead women's studies programs on women and development, and to be inspired again by that glorious lake. My institute took place in the Mayan village of San Marcos, a half hour's ride from Panajachel, the main town on the lake. My group rode in one of the local motor boats, called *lanchas,* that provide transportation around the lake. To board a *lancha,* our group members had to climb down several steps and maneuver down a steeply curved wooden hull to the passenger benches. Senior members were not happy. The *lancha* was delightful when the water was calm and a bit like a chicken bus when it was rough.

By 2008, Panajachel had become larger, less hippie, more touristy and somewhat tacky. The main street was lined with shops full of cheap souvenirs and had taco bars on every corner. I was delighted to get my group out of town and to a Mayan village that felt as if it belonged to the scenic natural environment. San Marcos had dirt paths crisscrossing it, friendly dogs and chickens wandering around, and tourist facilities mostly hidden behind stucco walls. At first, some group members found the village too primitive, but once they uncovered the cheerful restaurants, bars, and pensions, they felt right at home.

In actuality, San Marcos is an unusual combination of Mayan tradition and California counterculture. The village has been adopted by New Age types – health, nature and psychic devotees – who offer massage, yoga, tarot readings and other spiritual pursuits. The counterculture types and tourism providers coexist comfortably with the Mayans, who come down from the mountain where they live and grow coffee, to work in the village. One reason I chose San Marcos for my workshop was that many people in the village, Americans and Europeans, engaged in needed activities to help women and their families.

My group stayed in a pension right at the lake's edge, which was perfect for early morning meditation and night-time star gazing. Several women rose early to sit in lotus position on the dock and become one with the gently lapping water and towering volcanos before them. Our workshop took place in a lovely retreat center up the hill that provided meeting space, massage, and the best conceivable vegetarian meals.

I had suggested to my group members that they read

up on Guatemalan history before they came, but none took my advice. In my view, the U.S., given its past, nefarious involvement in the country, had a particular responsibility for Guatemala. I felt compelled to share the story with the group.

In 1954, the U.S. helped engineer a coup against the only progressive government Guatemala ever had in order to protect the interests of the United Fruit Company, the biggest business, landowner, and employer in the country. From then on, the U.S. supported right-wing governments dominated by the military and large Guatemalan landowners. The indigenous Mayans, 70 percent of the population, received no help at all. In the 1970s and 1980s, when Guatemalan farmers, students, and progressives began to protest the regime, the military, again condoned by the U.S., conducted a genocidal campaign against rural Mayans, both guerillas and civilians, wiping out whole villages and killing 200,000. Only when the military and guerillas agreed to a cease-fire did the U.S. speak out against the regime's massacres.

Fortunately, many international non-governmental organizations (NGOs) have stepped in to help the indigenous people of Guatemala. One group started with Guatemala City's gigantic garbage dump. In Antigua we learned about Safe Passage, an American NGO that assists children who spend their days scavenging the dump for recyclable materials. The children are exposed to poisonous toxins and dangerous pieces of metal and wood. My group stayed at a pension, run by Safe Passage, that donates its profits to buy food for families living in the dump and runs schools for the dump's children. The attention brought by Safe Passage ultimately forced the Guatemalan government to provide housing for the dump workers.

When, in the 1960s, the U.S. first designed development programs – for Guatemala and the rest of the developing world – its goal was making poor, rural countries more like the industrialized West. Plans emphasized building infrastructure – transportation, utilities, communications – and promoting corporate agriculture and industrialization. These programs made the rich of Guatemala richer but had no impact on poverty. From the late 1970s to the early 1990s, international development efforts changed course to focus on poverty, women's lives, and the environment, but these approaches failed to help Guatemala which was then in the midst of a civil war.

Sad to say, development not only failed to assist the indigenous people of Guatemala but, in fact, it harmed them. For example, while the government was constructing a beautiful airport to advance international trade and tourism, country roads deteriorated badly or simply washed away in the torrential summer rains. Poor people could make money only by emigrating to the U.S. or engaging in a rapidly expanding drug trade. Even child adoption became a racket as adoption agencies, aided by government officials providing false identity papers, frequently kidnaped indigenous children.

The only assistance given the indigenous people came from foreign NGOs trying to fill the gaps left by the

Guatemalan government. In San Marcos, I was greatly impressed by *Clinicas Naturista*, a clean and attractive naturopathic clinic, originally set up by a Swiss doctor and eventually run by an outspoken and committed American nurse/midwife. With a staff of 8 indigenous workers, the clinic treated many sick or pregnant women throughout the community, although not all since some women still turned to the local shaman. We learned from the American nurse that few indigenous women received any sex education before marriage and, given their ignorance and crowded living conditions, few experienced sexual gratification. Thus, while their health has improved, women endure sex solely to produce children.

Mayan women's greatest collective talent is their extraordinary weaving skill, but from San Marcos and other lake villages it was hard for women to get their work to the main tourist market in Panajachel. An Italian woman in San Marcos decided to create a weaving cooperative, *Luna Kakchiquel*, with a group of Mayan women from the village. The women were given weaving and natural dye courses and also language education in Spanish so they could communicate with tourists. *Luna Kakchiquel* both provides employment and encourages women to feel equal to the men of the village. When my women's group met with women in the cooperative, we asked if the village men supported their efforts. They laughed and said, "Fifty percent." Why only fifty percent, we wondered. They replied the men were afraid the women might take over!

I also met Susana, a phenomenal German woman, dark blond and lanky, who had lived in Guatemala for 15 years and had started a recycling program to clean San Marcos of tourist trash. This was a big task for a land in which 95 percent of rural people have no garbage collection and burn all their waste, even plastic. Susana came up with an ingenious solution to deal with half-liter plastic water bottles strewn around the village. She taught local kids to collect them and stuff them with plastic bags and wrappers, giving a reward of a marble for each filled bottle. Then she used the bottles as construction material to build walls, eventually covering them with stucco.

"Do these buildings really stay up?" I asked.

"Oh, they are much better than the usual adobe bricks," Susana declared.

"Why?"

"Plastic bottle walls are durable and, of course, they are cheaper than cement blocks. Even more important, they are far more flexible. The highlands are subject to earthquakes and walls from plastic bottles protect people from natural disaster."

I was not surprised Susana won an award from the European Union for her creativity.

Finally, our group spent a day in Panajachel with an Australian woman who had moved to Guatemala in the 1970s. She eventually started an NGO, Mayan Families, that supported hundreds of children from destitute families by paying their school fees and purchasing their uniforms. Without some education, the children were destined to suffer the same lives of scarcity their mothers endured. Mayan Families also sustained widows or abandoned women by providing food, clothes, medical exams, furniture and water filters. The Director took us to see typical poor people's homes – bare wooden shacks with tin roofs, mud floors, one overhead lightbulb, a toilet and stove outside, and often a flowery plant growing outside the shack. Donated stoves used bricks rather than wood to sustain heat, an important advance in appropriate technology.

My women's studies programs concluded at the wondrous site of Tikal in northern Guatemala where we had a chance to learn about the ancient Mayans. Our group flew from Guatemala City to Flores, an island town on a lake about 40 miles from Tikal. Flores was a delightful tourist town with small hotels, pensions, tourist shops and numerous restaurants, many of which provide views of the lake and surrounding greenery. From Flores, the van ride to Tikal took us through a scrubby landscape that made me wonder how the ancient Mayans managed to settle in that inhospitable environment . I soon found out.

Tikal National Park, a UNESCO World Heritage Site,

stretches across 220 square miles. Covered by thick foliage of kapok, cedar and mahogany trees, it was beautiful in a very different way from Lake Atitlan. Its wildlife included howler monkeys, unusual small mammals like the racoon-like coatimundi and many kinds of tropical birds. The thickness of the jungle explained why Tikal's ruins were unknown and undiscovered for hundreds of years. From the edge of the densely forested park, it was a twenty-minute drive to the ancient city center which extends over six miles and once included 3000 structures, all carved from the soft limestone of the area. Tikal's major architectural structures were constructed on high mounds, linked by causeways that effectively spanned swampy ground.

Tikal flourished in the Classic Maya Period, from 250 - 900 A.D., when the city was filled with temples (many over 200 feet tall), royal palaces, administration buildings, ball courts, platforms and carved monuments. Outside the center city was a vast community of 23 square miles, most of which has not been cleared or excavated. Estimates of the population of the city center range from 10,000 to 90,000, with possibly 400,000 in the surrounding unexcavated residential area. A stunning number. Tikal was a major metropolis.

Ancient Mayan civilization is known not only for its architecture, but also for its science -- calculating time (a 13 month yearly calendar), charting the universe, writing, artistic design and stone sculpture. This all occurred at the time Europe was going through the Dark Ages! I asked myself how a city of such size could survive without a source of water – no river or springs – and learned that, for all their liquid needs, ancient Mayans collected seasonal rainwater. Rather than depending on natural sinkholes, *cenotes*, they built ten huge reservoirs and used canals to transport water from one section of the city to another. Irrigation in the fertile upland soil made agriculture possible; enough food was produced in the jungle to feed hundreds of thousands. Scientific knowledge made life in the Peten not only possible but highly developed!

Knowing that ancient Mayans managed development

on such a phenomenal scale, I became fascinated by the collapse of their civilization. At the end of the tenth century A.D., Mayan cities and communities disappeared, eventually camouflaged by the green blanket of the jungle. How did this happen? Some archeologists argue the area suffered a long-term drought, driving the population out to find more fertile land. Others hypothesize that endemic warfare in the region produced high numbers of refugees that strained Tikal's resources, although there is little evidence of warfare in Mayan carvings or art. Whether disaster was brought by warring males, environmental shifts, or both, the civilization ultimately disappeared.

Contemplating the collapse of the ancient Mayas, I felt, once again, profound sadness that a civilization had expanded beyond its means without regard for sustainability. Development outpaced and exhausted natural resources. While today our environmental and women's movements emphasize renewal and controlled growth, our leadership, predominantly male, drives us down paths to self-destruction. The Ancient Maya have much to teach us if we only listen.

A comparison of ancient and contemporary Mayas was, for me, shocking. One of the world's great civilizations has become a downtrodden community. Modern Guatemala's development has lagged terribly – it ranks 122 out of 192 on the UN's Human Development Index, the worst in Central and South America. While the wealthy elite of Guatemala prosper, the Mayan majority has no prospects except agriculture on small family lots and low-level jobs in tourism.

I ask myself what form of development would benefit the Mayan people, especially the women, and, of course, indigenous people in other countries. The NGOs I encountered were providing essential services but were not changing the class structure or overcoming poverty. Yet, without major land distribution, poor indigenous farmers have few possibilities.

That is not something outsiders can make happen. To

gain land, Mayans themselves must push vigorously for social and economic reform and a reformist government must win office, a government that is supported, not overthrown, by the U.S. That might necessitate a radical revolt in Guatemala which, if anything like the 1980s disastrous civil war, is unlikely to succeed.

Does small-scale development fostered by NGOs have an impact on Mayan life? Certainly, NGOs are making them healthier and more literate. Modest economic development will make indigenous people more active consumers, although not necessarily producers. And, for a couple of lucky individuals, NGOs might, through education, open doors of opportunity presently wedged shut.

At the same time that foreign NGOs provide humanitarian services, foreign developers seek to commercialize, perhaps even destroy, beautiful Lake Atitlan and many other pristine indigenous areas. To give just one terrible example, I heard talk of bringing casinos to nature's jewel, Lake Atitlan, in order to draw crowds of gamblers. Likewise, today many women in towns are running shops filled with second-hand American clothes rather than learning the weaving techniques that make Guatemalan fabric admired across the world. Commercial development of these kinds alone will inevitably expose Mayan people to values and practices that are inimical and weaken ties to traditional culture.

Can <u>any</u> model of externally-imposed development work for indigenous peoples? I doubt it. To preserve indigenous cultures, whether in Guatemala, Australia or elsewhere, change has to come from within, not outside. And Mayan women, like those in San Marcos, must be willing to "take over" leadership – what their men feared – so that development incorporates their needs. Finally, taking a lesson from the Mayan world a millennium ago, progress of any kind must rest on the practice of sustainability or advancing civilization will again, tragically, disappear.

Unraveling India

India, the first destination on my Asia travel from 2004 to 2009, was a complicated and confusing place that was also at times rewarding and touching. When I chose India as the location for my 60th birthday celebration, some friends assumed I was going to chant in an ashram and kneel at the feet of a guru with a long white beard, but I was not on a spiritual journey. I simply wanted to sample a bit of Indian culture and learn something about India's patterns of social and economic development. When I did pray on that journey, my prayers had nothing to do with finding nirvana but with finding a train that would depart and arrive on time. That never happened.

Although Jim and I were not on a pilgrimage, our arrival in Delhi was strangely auspicious. Adopting our preferred style of travel, we avoided the extremes – no upscale tourist packages and no backpacking. We traveled modestly, encountered (admittedly middle class) Indian travelers, and experienced aspects of real Indian life. Using <u>Lonely Planet</u>, I reserved an inexpensive hotel located near Delhi's middle traffic ring, which I assumed, for no reason at all, was a decent neighborhood. The hotel had a Web site which led me, again mistakenly, to believe it was relatively modern.

We flew to Delhi on the cheapest available flight which brought us from California to India by way of Rome. When, depleted by travel fatigue, we finally got a taxi in Delhi's chaotic airport and arrived at our hotel, I was dismayed to find the street in front littered with garbage and what appeared to be sleeping bodies and a man urinating against a nearby building.

Our small, poorly lit hotel had rooms jutting in strange directions off a twisting staircase. A young man carried our suitcases up five landings to the roof where our room had a double bed that took up most of the small space and a bathroom the size of a tiny closet. With no windows, the room was dank and dreary. Since it was too late at night to find another hotel, we sank down on the bed to wait for morning.

Jim flicked on the large, old-fashioned television, our one "modern" convenience, to see if it worked. We were stunned to see ocean waves the height of two-story buildings crashing along the Tamil Nadu coast, pulverizing piers and sucking fishing boats out to sea. On that day, December 26, 2004, the Indian Ocean tsunami, after destroying Banda Aceh in Indonesia, had traveled 1500 miles across the Bay of Bengal, to devastate the east coast of the Indian subcontinent and Sri Lanka. Watching the mind-boggling destruction of nature at work, we ached for the thousands of victims and felt intensely grateful for our paltry, but firmly grounded, hotel far from the ocean.

News of the tsunami pounded us for several days.

The next morning we expected to meet Indians torn by grief, but the people we encountered seemed surprisingly matter of fact. Our hotel clerk explained that Tamil Nadu was far from Delhi and, unless someone had family in the affected area, the tsunami was just another tragedy of nature. That was my first taste of Indian fatalism.

Jim and I decided we might as well sightsee since we were safe and had come a long way to see India. As we walked along the street to find a taxi, we passed a dingy travel agency advertising cars and drivers. We'd been told this form of transportation was inexpensive and well worth it for circumventing hordes of people on the streets. We ended up hiring a driver, Thakur, who drove a musty, old gray, Indian-made Tata sedan and seemed glad for our business. For two days Thakur, short, rather handsome with a dark mustache and thick eyebrows, transported us to the main sights of Delhi – imposing Hindu temples, the Red Fort, grand colonial-style government buildings along wide avenues. My favorite stop was the wild and colorful bazaar of Old Delhi with narrow alleys smelling pungently of frying *samosas* and boasting hundreds of tiny shops selling saris, fake antiques, and gold bangles.

There I had my first extended encounter with beggars. They were everywhere. Our guidebook warned us to walk by and make no eye contact, but I couldn't do that. It was hardest for me to ignore cripples, often missing two or three limbs, possibly from leprosy. I loaded my pockets with small change. I realized I needed criteria for giving or I would be besieged all day long. I decided to give only to old women, mothers with babies, and cripples. When dropping money in the cripples' outstretched hands, I tried to glance only at their faces and avoid, partly out of horror, partly out of sadness, looking at their bodies.

By the time we finished our two-day city tour, we had happily hired Thakur, a cheerful man and safe driver, to take us for five days to nearby Agra and then far west to Rajasthan. When he picked us up, he was accompanied, in the front seat by his son, 13 year old Sunil, a slim cocoa-skinned boy. Thakur was relieved we had no objection to having Sunil come along. Later that day, seeing the Taj Mahal through Sunil's eyes made all the difference. Without him, it would have felt like a postcard-type experience, magnificent but previously imprinted on my brain. With Sunil, once we got through the gate and he saw for his first time India's pearly gift to world civilization, he stopped in place and stared as if in a trance. At that moment, a humble Indian youth became a fiercely proud citizen of the planet.

Our eight-hour drive to Jaipur, the capital of Rajasthan, took us past stunning, bright yellow fields of rapeseed, women farmers in rainbow-colored saris working in the fields, scattered mud huts, and a stream of villages where garbage, ravaged by stray dogs, clogged every drain and street corner. We probably saw more devastation that one day than most American tourists in luxury coaches see on their entire trips. It hit me visually that desperate poverty was as much, or more, a condition of rural life as it was in congested and polluted cities.

Thakur was always ready with answers to my questions. Despite their gorgeous colors, the saris on clotheslines were perhaps the only article of clothing, or one of two, the women owned. Garbage was just one aspect of the complete lack of services – no running water, electricity, schools or clinics – that characterizes rural India. Even the rapeseed seemed less beautiful when we understood that it, or other products, typically provide 600 million Indian farmers and their families only one or two dollars a day.

Rajasthan, India's largest province, is mostly desert. Jaipur is known as the Pink City because it was painted pink in 1853 to welcome the visiting Prince of Wales. I was expecting the color of a rosebud and was disappointed to find the huge palace and state buildings more a reddish-tan. With a roof view of the city and decent food in the restaurant, we found our budget bed and breakfast, also courtesy of <u>Lonely Planet,</u> far superior to our Delhi hotel. Sightseeing included the royal buildings and, outside the city, a mountain fort and palace with exquisite buildings and tile work. At the fort, we took an elephant ride with Sunil who seemed to find the elephant as exciting as the Taj Mahal. He bounded off the platform onto the elephant seat. Jim and I took it a lot more slowly.

During our stay, we managed some shopping since Jaipur specializes in semi-precious stones and wool carpets. The rug factory had floor-to-ceiling piles of rugs. Thakur, who assured us the factory was the best in town, told us ahead of time he would get a small commission. He urged us not feel any pressure to buy. I was pleased by his honesty and, after many cups of tea and fierce bargaining, we purchased a blue and rose flowered rug for our dining room, happy to know a small amount of the cost would go to Thakur. The rug dealer asked us which day we would like the rug delivered to our home in California. While I couldn't imagine such precision for a delivery six weeks later and halfway around the world, the rug arrived on the designated day. Blessings to Thakur, the factory, and Federal Express.

Jaipur gave me my first one-on-one lesson regarding the plight of Indian women. I had a pre-arranged meeting with an upper class Muslim woman who ran an organization out of her home that helped Muslim women with literacy, jobs at home, and domestic violence. The NGO leader was elegantly clothed in a brocade dress, *pashmina* shawl, and intricate gold earrings. She proudly introduced her two sons who were attending college. My new friend Raja informed me the Hindu-Muslim divide in India extends to local government, and Muslim women in Jaipur, being in the minority, had little access to educational and work programs that were provided to Hindu women. Further, most Muslim women are, by cultural tradition, restricted to their neighborhoods and rarely attend school. Raja's organization taught them literacy and embroidery, work that could be done at home. It also provided shelters for women who were beaten by their husbands, unfortunately reaching only a tiny proportion of women in need of such assistance.

I knew before I came to India that Americans have a distorted view of the country. In the media we hear about Bollywood, India's high tech boom, and the outsourcing of U.S. jobs, and we come away with a false impression. The unnoticed poor in India are so badly off that, according to the UN's 2009 Human Development Index, India ranked 134 out of 182 countries worldwide. From the data, I understood that Indian women fare the worst. While they had a slightly higher life expectancy than men (although still low at 64 years of age), they were not even two-thirds as literate. Only 88 percent of girls attended school and for fewer years than boys. Perhaps the data that concerned me the most referred to India's "missing women." An estimated 1.5 million fewer girls were born each year than would be expected based on demographics. Because parents so strongly prefer boys, many middle class families aborted female fetuses. Poor families often committed female infanticide or so neglected girl children that they died before the age of five.

In Indian bookshops I searched for material to explain the lack of rural development, especially the factors that kept women so far behind men. I picked up two books by Amartya Sen, India's Nobel Prize winning economist who has devoted much of his career to development. Sen argued persuasively that in recent years India has focused on economic liberalization for the urban middle classes without providing basic educational and health services for the rural masses, thereby dramatically exacerbating the gap between rich and poor. He pointed out that only one section of India, the southern state of Kerala, had exceeded China, as well as every other area of India, in terms of social development. What a fascinating puzzle. I had to learn why.

On the way to Kerala, Jim and I stopped off in the state of Karnataka to see the high tech center of Bangalore and visit the former royal state of Mysore. Bangalore looked and felt like a small American city with modern office buildings, supermarkets and shopping malls, many new condo high rises, and no native atmosphere. Only the chaotic street traffic with luxury cars skirting around rickshaws gave any hint of India. In search of fruit, I went into a supermarket and found apples and oranges covered by plastic wrap. I had the eerie feeling I was back in California. Sadly, the invasion of Indian and foreign "geeks" have pushed Bangalore's local people to shacks at the city's edge. Food prices have gone so high that long-time local residents are struggling to eat. Just below the surface of admired high tech development, the excluded, once managing, now scramble to survive.

To get to Kerala from Bangalore, Jim and I took our first Indian train ride. The station was swarmed with people, some camped on the lobby floor with bedding and gas burners. When we figured out our train track, we had to climb a long flight of stairs, cross over a passageway, and descend to our platform. There were no escalators or elevators, only skinny porters in pajama-like clothing who tried to seize our bags and carry them for us. We tried to give our bags to a porter who looked a bit younger and stronger, but a competitor, thinner, wrinkled and barefoot, pushed him aside and swung one of our heavy suitcases onto his head. I was even more dismayed when he swung the second suitcase on top of the first. Short of breath and straining from the weight of my small carry-on bag, I followed him as he bounded up the stairs, across the passageway and down the second flight. We paid double for his heroic effort.

Our train arrived in the Bangalore station a half hour late, then sat for another half hour, then slowly limped through the countryside. Everyone in our first class car was sleeping or eating. We ordered tea and chapatis from a rumpled young man, silver bowls strung across his shoulders, who was plying the train. With our train more and more behind schedule, we consumed a dinner of potato chips, then more chapatis, and at last a blessed orange still in its skin. I worried we would get to Trivandrum so late we wouldn't find transportation to our hotel. No worries, a spectacled young man on the next seat told me, "There are always taxis." On a later journey, when we arrived at our destination at four in the morning, I learned he was right. If there is money to be made by meeting a train, no matter how late, Indian taxi drivers will be there.

I quickly fell in love with tropical Kerala, the southwestern province of India bordering the Arabian

Sea. It offered a stunning contrast to the desert terrain of Rajasthan – deep green countryside studded by clusters of palm trees, smooth beige beaches dotted with fishing villages, warm azure ocean with gentle waves. After India's dense, blaring, crowded cities, I was at peace by the ocean, on the holiday I'd begun to yearn for. We headed to a town patronized by Indian vacationers and foreign backpackers. Lunch on the beach was sold by basket-laden women in sarongs who cut up luscious fresh papayas and mangoes before our eyes.

From Trivandrum, we made an overnight excursion in a slowly gliding houseboat over the Kerala backwaters, consisting of 1500 kilometers of canals along 38 rivers. Our picturesque wooden boat, seventy feet long and five feet wide with a curved woven bamboo roof, had a lounge deck in the bow with comfortable bamboo chairs and a compact interior bedroom and bath. Our boatman poled by verdant rice fields, tiny villages, and minute waterside huts. As pleasant as the ride was, I wouldn't recommend bathing or doing laundry, as many locals did, in the algae-laden canals. Our boatman cooked us meals in the small kitchen in the stern, and once he knew we liked chilies, he put out a fiery tomato chutney with every dish. We were close to paradise. The placid waters, shorelines fringed by palm trees, and fields of emerald rice stalks put Kerala's back waters high on my list of the world's most restful places.

Our last stop in Kerala was the city of Kochi (formerly Cochin), a major seaport with a harbor full of tall sails billowing over traditional, but sleek, fishing boats. Cochin was the first European settlement in India, settled by Portuguese in 1503. Long before the Portuguese, however, came Jews from Palestine, perhaps 2500 years ago. The Jewish community, the largest in India, was oppressed by the Catholic Portuguese but tolerated by the Dutch Protestants who took over the city in 1660. Today, in the old city, there is still a charming area known as Jew Town that is filled with antique shops full of ceramics, art, and carved wooden furniture. While Jew Town still has a couple of synagogues and Jewish street names, most

Indian Jews have emigrated to Israel and only a few remain in Kochi. Even as a secular Jew, I felt more comfortable there than in anywhere else in India, feeling a connection through my own religious heritage.

Along with tropical beauty, Kerala gave me some valuable lessons on Indian women. Reading Amartya Sen's book, *Indian Development,* answered many of my questions about women in Kerala. To my amazement, they equaled men in literacy (close to 100 percent) and had a life expectancy six years longer than men's. And there were no missing women. Women made up a higher proportion than men in the population,1040 females to 1000 males, as would be expected demographically. I wondered how women in Kerala had advanced so dramatically compared to the rest of India.

Three historical factors explained this phenomenon. When, a millennium ago, before the people of Kerala encountered Europeans or Muslims (Muslim invaders never went so far south), the indigenous Nayars lived in a matrilineal and matrilocal society. Inheritance was passed through the female line and families lived in female-headed households. Nayar society endowed women with high social status, and even back in the 16th to 18th centuries, a few Nayar women acquired literacy.

A second factor promoting female literacy was European missionary activity in the 19th and early 20th centuries. While Catholics missionaries proselytized further north and adhered to local custom, in Kerala Protestant missionaries from England and Holland reached out to oppressed castes and included girls in their classes.

The final factor benefitting women in Kerala was the dominance of the Communist Party from the end of World War II until today. When Kerala became a state in the mid-1950s, the Communists came to power on a program of land reform and redistribution, food subsidies, and health and education to all. They successfully mobilized women, and literate mothers produced literate children.

By the 1990s, all the girls of Kerala were educated and immunized.

When in Trivandrum, I was invited by a professional colleague who worked on AIDS prevention to give a couple of lectures to university classes on the U.S. women's movement. Afterward, I chatted with women students, backpacks over their saris, who were studying government and law. I asked them about their career aspirations and was surprised that, once they married and started having children, they all planned to stop working. Since there is no shortage of household help in India, they obviously had other reasons for giving up their careers. The law students told me they were following custom – Indian mothers stay at home with their children and do not work, even in socially developed Kerala!

I was astounded and responded that many mothers in Mumbai and New Delhi pursue careers. The students informed me that, outside India's sophisticated cities, working mothers were severely criticized unless they worked out of necessity. The students also said that, once married, they would go out in the evenings only with their husbands. I suddenly understood why, on my journey, I had never seen women out socializing on their own.

This conversation put women's impressive accomplishments in Kerala in perspective. While girls and younger women were encouraged intellectually and professionally, once they began families, they were relegated to traditional roles. Whatever status middle class Indian women achieved, their professional lives and accomplishments were, with only a few exceptions, circumscribed by family expectations. How could one account for these ongoing restrictions in a country trying so hard to modernize? I came to see gender as India's unnamed and invisible caste.

Our last stop in India was Goa, a former Portuguese colony until Indian troops attacked in 1961 and Portugal retreated. The Portuguese presence explained the plethora of colonial-style buildings downtown and the long-time fondness of Europeans for beach vacations in Goa. The hotels were a bit fancier than in Kerala and the food a bit more varied, but I preferred Kerala for its mix of beaches, lovely back waters, and Kochi on the sea.

One day on the beach, I was stretched out with a book when a woman in a sarong, who was selling bead necklaces, stopped at my beach chair. She dropped onto the sand, we chatted awhile, and I bought several necklaces for gifts. I asked about her business. She complained that the young fellow hovering nearby took too much from her profits. When I asked why she gave the young man money, she told me he controlled the beach even though it was a public facility. Any women working there had to pay him off. I then asked if the men selling ice cream on the beach also paid him off and she sadly shook her head. At that point the young man came over, yelled at the woman to get back to work and stalked away. Distressed by yet one more example of female oppression, I gave her some additional rupees and said, "This is for you, not him." Smiling at me, she hid the money in her bra.

When my birthday came, I luxuriated in a hot oil massage at the beach and Jim and I enjoyed a barbecued shrimp dinner with a touch of the bubbly. Despite my "big day," I felt subdued. India had been such an intense experience that my birthday paled in comparison. Instead of celebrating my own existence, I felt somber at the recurring thought of millions of Indians women, whose whole existence was punishing and fragile. It was hard to get in an upbeat mood.

Then it was time to fly back to Delhi and on home. There would be no more late trains, no more disturbing street beggars, and, thank heavens, no more Indian food. While I had started out enjoying Indian cuisine, after a month of *paneer*, kebabs and *naan,* I longed for a steak and fresh salad.

On our last day in New Delhi, Thakur gave me a gift I had been wishing for – a visit to the home of an average, middle class, Indian. He invited Jim and me to lunch and to meet the rest of his family. We took a taxi to the outskirts of Delhi to a neighborhood of two-story buildings with unpaved streets and scattered piles of garbage. Thakur had moved to New Delhi from his family's farm and built his house when the area was still agricultural fields. Urban services had not arrived in the area as fast as new residents.

Thakur and his family lived on the second floor, above a shop he rented out. There were only three small rooms in the apartment – one for Thakur and his wife which doubled as a living room, a kitchen, and a room for the three children with a laptop computer on a desk. We were invited to sit on the bed in the main room, across from a television, that served as a couch. Thakur's wife served food – chapatis again, rice, and dal – on the two china plates the family owned. The family sat around us on low wooden stools and watched us eat, claiming they had eaten before. We spoke in English with Thakur translating for his wife. Thakur insisted on pouring us beer and happily drank with us. When I needed the toilet, I discovered a hall closet with a hole in the ground. The most appealing part of the house was the roof where the family slept in summertime and where we had a view of the area that excluded the dirty streets.

After exchanging gifts and making our farewells, I reflected on Thakur's status and lifestyle. He owned his own home, took in rent from below, sent his kids to private neighborhood schools, and was saving to buy his own car rather than work as a salaried driver. He had purchased a computer and cell phone. All this made him middle class. Nonetheless, his neighborhood was rundown and his living space, small. Most of all, his neighborhood lacked basic services – clean, paved streets, plumbing, a touch of green – that we in developed countries consider standard.

I recalled a conversation I'd had with Thakur several weeks earlier. A relatively progressive man, he was ambitious for his children, at least, for the boys. After high school, the boys would go to post-secondary training of some kind. Thakur's daughter would remain at home with her mother to learn to sew and embroider. Why not further education for her, I asked. Because it would reflect badly on the family to have a daughter in the marketplace or in the world of work.

Thakur was, no doubt, an Indian success story, and his sons will also succeed. The best Thakur's daughter can hope for is to marry in an approved match. Thakur will spend an extraordinary amount of money on her wedding and perhaps his daughter will end up happy, but she will have no life outside her family.

We stayed in touch with Thakur who called us from time to time on his cell phone. His son Sunil occasionally sent an email and his English spelling was improving. Part of me regretted I could not do more for Thakur, although I always sent him money with friends going to New Delhi. Another part of me knew he was delighted to have two American friends.

After one month of travel, I doubted I would return to India. Seeing and learning a great deal more would still not amount to "unraveling" the place, its values and customs. Kerala stood out as India's exception. For similar social development to occur in other Indian states, it would require a left-wing redistribution of wealth as occurred in Kerala after World War II, and that, despite urging from a Nobel Prize-winning economist, is not likely to happen. Likewise, most Indian women, even those who attain education, remain restricted by custom, subject to ingrained patriarchy.

Perhaps the aspect of India most troublesome for me was the reckless pursuit of prosperity by the urban rich, while the rural poor, 600 million of them, remained deprived and neglected. While a terrible class divide also exists in the U.S., India's extremes are all-encompassing and ill-attended, and very hard to witness.

Gaping at China

When Richard Nixon made his historic trip to Communist China in 1972, he opened the doorway for Americans curious about the world's most populous nation. I made the trip several years later in 1979, traveling with an American women's group hosted by the All China Women's Federation. We were definitely on an official visit – lots of formal sessions with women officials and no freedom to wander – and China was definitely still Communist.

I remember the signs of totalitarianism. When we went out on tour, our suitcases were inspected in our hotel rooms. We had guessed that would be the case and, consequently, packed our clothes each morning in a particular way that was hard to replicate. We always found our luggage arranged slightly differently when we returned to our rooms. In another form of this game, we stuck a hair across the top of a closed suitcase and it was never there when we got back. Nothing was ever missing from our luggage. It was just fun playing James Bond.

Mao declared the Cultural Revolution over in 1969, but it wasn't until 1976 that the Gang of Four was arrested. Our group encountered the legacy of the Cultural Revolution when, in a park in Shanghai, we met a lovely woman, her hair tied up in a knot and her thin face more elongated than most Chinese. She said she'd once been an English teacher.

"Friends," said the teacher, "I wonder if you have any books in English you have finished reading?"

"Yes," we replied with excitement. "They are on the bus. Let us get them for you."

"Oh, no," she rushed to say. "Someone might see you

giving them to me. Could you drop them out the window when your bus leaves?"

I felt anxious a snitch or guard might see her but we dropped the books and, fortunately, there didn't seem to be anyone around to report her.

During our sightseeing, I remember hearing the Communist party line over and over again. Our young female guide didn't know we had one group member who knew Mandarin and who eventually provided us real translations rather than propaganda mouthed by the guide. As just one example, when we visited a tea commune, we asked a young woman on a tea-picking brigade why only women worked as pickers. She responded that women's hands were more delicate. Her answer was nonsensical, probably a bit of propaganda she'd been taught. So we asked why, if women had more delicate hands, all the surgeons of China were men. Stunned, she replied she had never thought of that. The guide translated her response as "(W)omen don't want to be surgeons."

I also recall vividly what it was like to be in a backward

country. We had dreamed of eating scrumptious Chinese food every day, but our meals were overcooked, laden with soggy cabbage, bland and oily. Our guest houses were often only half-finished with exposed wires running along bathroom floors. The dust was so bad during August that several group members succumbed to bronchial conditions. I accompanied our group leader to visit our sick companions in a hospital that, more than anything, resembled a morgue with inert bodies curled up in womb-like positions on rows of beds. Happily, our friends recovered.

Of course, there were fantastic sites in China, such as the Forbidden City in Beijing, the Shanghai waterfront, and, in Xian, the newly excavated terra cotta soldiers and horses in the tomb of the first Qin emperor that were discovered by a farmer plowing a field. At the end of that trip, I sensed I would go back to China someday. When I finally did return 30 years later, I knew it would be a different country – not very Communist and very developed. Still, it was a shock to discover just how different.

In May, 2009, Jim and I made our trip to China, thanks to an invitation from friends living and working in Shanghai who had kindly offered us their guest room. Friends from our Hawaii days, Brenda was working as Director of the American Chamber of Commerce while Larry, a law professor, consulted with Chinese law firms. Both our friends had advanced degrees in Chinese Studies and spoke excellent Chinese, making them the perfect hosts.

Mao would certainly have gaped at Shanghai Airport, gigantic yet well-organized, crammed with duty-free luxury goods from around the world. In the taxi to our friends' apartment, I was stunned by what seemed to be thousands, and actually were thousands, of high-rise apartment and office buildings, almost all built in the last two decades. Naturally, a city of over 20 million people must have places for people to live. Even so, the visual impact of so many buildings, looking new but crowded together with no visible green space, made my mouth drop open. It was like seeing a city made from Leggos.

The place to see ancient Chinese art is the Shanghai Museum, now housed in an elegant building opened in 1996. The museum collection of bronzes, ceramics, paintings, and calligraphy contains around 120,000 pieces. This number doesn't compare to the 3 million objects belonging to St. Petersburg's Hermitage, but all of the Shanghai Museum's works are native to the country. When I saw what China had created over millennia, I understood how that culture had reigned as the world's most advanced civilization, at least before the European Industrial Revolution.

After seeing the museum's breathtaking ceramics, I felt an urge to go shopping, not for expensive antiques, but for pieces perhaps a century old or for copies that are nonetheless beautifully made. My guidebook was pretty informative about flea markets in the Yu Yuan shopping district. Jim and I went to a weekend market in a three-story building that had individual, semi-permanent stalls on the first floor, and two upper floors for out-of-town Chinese who spread sheets on the cement with their "treasures" arranged on top.

I found it hard to make my way through the narrow aisles and fix on anything in particular because there was so much to see. I made the mistake of saying I was looking for a statue of Kwan Yin, the goddess of mercy and healing, a strong women's symbol. Within two minutes, I was besieged by eight or ten salespeople, shouting in Chinese, clutching statues and waving them in my face. I finally bought one, thinking my purchase would drive the other salespeople away, but they persisted. By morning's end, I had found some lovely ceramics and roll-up screens that I bargained for in sign language. Then I had to buy an additional carry-on bag to carry my treasures home.

I had no interest or funds for the upscale stores along Nanjing Road, the super luxury district, but I did a lot of window shopping. I was awed by the miracle mile of designer and high-end stores. You could go inside a shop and buy a $25,000 Rolex watch or sneak outside and

buy a five dollar copy that actually ticked, although I'm
not sure for how long. I wandered through a number of
malls, expecting to see only foreigners, but discovered, to
my surprise, that many of the customers were Chinese
and always in Western clothes. Where had all this wealth
come from? Our friends explained that in the post-Mao
period there was nothing to buy, so the Chinese, who
seem to be genetically thrifty, saved their money. In 2009,
it was estimated Chinese consumers had $800 million in
savings and, suddenly, hordes of goods to choose from.
While, being Chinese, they were unlikely to become
spendthrifts, they could, from time to time, purchase
long-desired expensive items.

Besides shopping and taking in Chinese art, the most
compelling sight for me in Shanghai was revisiting the
Bund (from Urdu for "embankment"), the promenade
running along the western bank of the Huangpu River.
When I was there in 1979, the Bund, in the historic
International Settlement, consisted of numerous grand,
colonial-style banks and trading companies, homes

and foreign consulates, fronted by a leafy park that stretched along the river. In 2009, the Bund was under reconstruction for the 2010 Shanghai World Expo, with tunnels being cut for traffic so the waterfront would be free of cars. The colonial buildings were still there, but the junks and houseboats once cruising on the crowded river were gone.

On either side of the historic Bund, one extraordinary skyscraper after another has sprung up. One downtown building had an architectural space like a hole at the top that was wide enough to allow a 747 airplane to pass through. At night, the new buildings were adorned with streams of colored lights, a seeming combination of Christmas and Carnival. When viewed from a tourist cruise, the waterfronts and glittering reflections of light on the river, made me feel I was immersed in a brilliant Impressionist painting.

The Expo 2010 story illustrated for me the differences in style and economic wherewithal between China and the U.S. In imperial style, the Shanghai government named the Chinese Pavilion the Oriental Crown. Shanghai, working hard to make Expo even more impressive than the 2008 Olympics in Beijing, spent $45 billion on the site located on the eastern, or Pudong, side of the river. In response to past criticism for the excessive energy consumed by Shanghai's skyscrapers, Shanghai had made Expo's theme "Better Life, Better City" and was pushing energy efficiency and sustainable building practices.

At Expo, every guest country was invited to build a pavilion to promote its achievements. Our American friends told us that, for some time, the U.S. was unable to come up with the $60 or $70 million necessary to build its pavilion, in part because the U.S. Congress has forbidden using public monies for such endeavors. There was gloom that U.S. private interests would never come up with the funds. At last, the U.S. financial sector, urged by Secretary of Stated Clinton, came to the rescue. Whatever the US pavilion ultimately looks like, it will pale in comparison with the gigantic constructions funded by Chinese public monies.

After a few days, tired of Shanghai's economic boom, I began to long for something with more Chinese character and was ready to make excursions to historic cities outside Shanghai. To go to Hangzhou and Suzhou, we hired a guide and decided to travel by train, both to experience the Chinese train system and to save money on a car and driver. The new trains were exceptional – high speed, clean, with signs in English and Chinese providing arrival times, stations and outdoor weather reports. Best of all, the trains left exactly on the minute.

In 1979, I had seen Hangzhou's huge and peaceful lake, surrounded by a lovely natural park, but it was quite different the second time. Thirty years later, the lake was mobbed by Chinese tourists who left no possibility for serenity. While I am delighted the Chinese are able to afford tourism and see their own natural wonders, their sheer numbers, all following a guide's hoisted red flag, changed the quality of the sightseeing experience. For us, the only delightful part of visiting Hangzhou was stopping at an out-of-town tea plantation where there were no other visitors, Chinese or foreign, and where we could enjoy a presentation on the area's famous green tea and come home with samples.

Our next excursion brought us to Suzhou, famous for its canals, homes with gardens, and silk factories. A ride through the canals was pleasant and photogenic. The homes were beautifully landscaped, although China's beloved boulders of perforated rock, transported from a sacred lake in the interior, failed to move me. The silk factory was impressive – silk making is so labor intensive! The reasonable prices in the showroom made Suzhou a fine place to shop for gifts although I could have found the same things in the larger cities if I'd known where to go.

The best part of the excursions was getting to know our female guide, Flora (all guides choose Western names to make life easy for their clients). Flora was willing to answer, in good English, all our questions about life in China and seemed quite candid in her responses. She lived at least an hour's drive outside downtown Shanghai and, with no car, had to commute hours to and from work on public transportation. When I asked her if she wouldn't rather live in a small city with less of a commute, she looked horrified and said, "Shanghai is where everything happens. This is the fashion center of China." And her clothing – black leggings, a white spaghetti strap shirt, and royal blue hip length sweater with dolman sleeves – was quite fashionable.

Flora told us about living with her boyfriend, also a guide, and planning, in capitalist fashion, to marry him once he had set up his own tour business. She was upset about the one-child policy, telling us that, under Shanghai regulations, she would be allowed as an only child to have two children if she also married an only child.

"Unfortunately my boyfriend has a brother," she said.

"Is that a serious problem?"

"Oh, yes. If I want two children, I need to find a different boyfriend. My boyfriend understands why I might not marry him."

I was struck that having two children had more value for Flora than her feelings for any particular mate. She assured me all her friends felt the same way.

Back in Shanghai, Flora urged us to go to an inexpensive Chinese shopping district, known in local slang as Cheap Street. When Jim and I finally got there, we were overwhelmed by what seemed like thousands of stalls in one huge building. Fortunately, a young woman, who spoke basic English, attached herself to us and shepherded us around so I could find the shirts I wanted without being hassled by all the saleswomen. I could imagine Flora bargaining away, but for us foreigners, obvious suckers, it was a challenge to shop. After a half hour, we gave our informal escort a tip that probably used up whatever savings we made, but she was worth it.

When the time came to leave for Beijing, we decided to go by overnight train. We didn't understand beforehand that our compartment was for four people and ended up sharing it with two pleasant young Chinese men. Of course, that meant we slept in our clothes in our berths.

Nonetheless, the train was a wonderful experience – fast, inexpensive compared to a flight, comfortable for my legs although not for six foot tall Jim's, with clean bathrooms and pleasant service. If only the US had a similar system.

Beijing's *hutongs* are old-time alleys that give the visitor a sense of what Beijing looked like centuries ago. I definitely wanted to stay in the *hutongs* rather than in an upscale Marriott or Sheraton. From the train station, our taxi driver had a bit of a problem finding the correct alley for our hotel even though we had the address written in Chinese. Finally, we pulled up to a charming two-story building with an outdoor courtyard where we could eat breakfast or have a cup of tea in the pleasant spring air.

We were given a room in the hotel's older section that smelled of poor plumbing. We switched to a more modern room that had better plumbing, but there's no place in the *hutong* area where you can fully escape the smells since the area was built long before modern plumbing and has never been upgraded. Many residents use public bathrooms located on the streets. When, occasionally, I found myself wandering down an alley holding my nose, I reminded myself I could have been staying downtown in a sanitized, ultra-modern Marriott and would have completely missed the old-style *hutong* atmosphere.

Other than the plumbing, the *hutongs* were a delight. The tree-lined streets were just wide enough to offer one-way passage for cars, which meant that strolling was comfortable and relaxed. Recently, the area has become rather hip with avant garde shops and charming cafes offering different national cuisines. At dinnertime, we never left the *hutongs* because we could always find a neighborhood restaurant – Thai, Indian, crepes – that we liked. One evening, Jim and I ventured to a back street and sat down in a local restaurant that had Chinese barbecue and no English speakers around. We ended up eating some delicious meat cooked on a hot pot in front of us full of boiling oil. We didn't recognize the meat. I prayed it wasn't dog.

All through our trip, Jim studied his small paperback

of Chinese characters in an effort to learn some of the language. I figured that in several weeks he would be able to pick up only a few characters, but since learning languages is Jim's passion, I said nothing. It turned out Jim taught himself about 200 characters. While not enough to have conversations, it was enough to ask simple directions. Jim was able to navigate us onto public buses to the Forbidden City and nearby parks then get us back to the *hutongs*. I was impressed. I asked him to learn the characters for dog and snake in order to avoid such dishes in non-English-speaking restaurants and, as far as I know, we warded off those two Chinese delicacies.

The historic sites of Beijing – the Forbidden City and Summer Palace – were just as impressive in 2010 as they were in 1979, but, again, a major change was the swarms of Chinese tourists. I spent a lot of time trying to escape the crowds. That was helped by a second major change, namely, the modernization of Chinese tourism. At the Forbidden City, for example, we were able to rent headsets and get a full introduction to the site at a distance from the crush of Chinese tourists. For me, perhaps the most exciting site in modern Beijing was Olympic City. The Bird's Nest stadium, crisscrossed outside by steel girders that made the building resemble a nest, was even more stunning in person than it was in photographs or on tv. I have heard the Chinese have not found a sufficient number of performances to fill the stadium, and I hope it doesn't become just one more Olympic has-been.

From Beijing we flew to the last stop on our tour, Guizhou, in southwestern China near the Laotian and Burmese borders, where many indigenous minority tribes – Hmong, Bouyi, Dong and Geija – are settled. Every visitor to China should at some point escape its gargantuan cities and visit the countryside. The Southwest had extremely beautiful cone-shaped green hills, rushing rivers, hillsides and valleys patterned with emerald rice paddies, and people often wearing traditional clothes that were brightly colored and beautifully embroidered. With our guide we visited Hmong communities, which the Han Chinese call Miao, while the indigenous prefer their non-Chinese name, Hmong, and are proud to have settled in the area millennia ago.

Guizhou province is a remote and, for China, underpopulated area with 39 million people, about the same as California. The average annual income is $1270, the lowest in all the country. Kaili, the city where we stayed, was remarkable for its lack of traffic and crowds, at least in comparison to Shanghai and Beijing. To add to the pleasure was the Szechuan food, spicy and full of chilies and tasty, unfamiliar vegetables. Dinners were accompanied by delicious, mildly intoxicating rice wines. Finally, although the region was known as the rainy mountains, we were blessed with sunshine.

Our guide, Lee, a Hmong preppy in button down shirts and well-cut jeans, was a good English speaker and proud of his ethnic traditions. We visited a well-preserved, traditional town, Xijiang, where we spent time at a health clinic, partly funded by our friends at the American Chamber of Commerce in Shanghai. We also took in a museum full of breathtaking embroidered and batik Hmong costumes. We stopped at the workshop of a local silversmith with a long drooping mustache who made delicate ornaments in the traditional style. I couldn't resist a little shopping and came home with a black blouse embroidered with yellow and orange spirals and filigree silver earrings.

Our last visit was to Zhenyuan, a town that has been a mountain trading center for 2000 years. Located on what is known as the Southern Silk Road, the town spans a river that was a transmission point for salt and silk coming west from Canton (now Guangzhou) and for local tea going further west to Tibet and India. The old town consisted of tall narrow buildings crowned and decorated with sculpture carved in the shape of dragons. Pedestrian bridges over the river were adorned with pagodas. From my hotel room balcony, I could drink in a magical sight, illuminated in the evening by colored lights.

If Guizhou is China's poorest region, I would never have known it. Many village homes had satellite dishes (costing about $25 each) and most people had mobile phones which cost very little to buy and use. Homes were small with earth floors, yet people were welcoming to strangers. They offered us tea, showed off their babies, and asked our guide questions about where we'd come from. Throughout Guizhou, there seemed to be a genuine effort to preserve minority culture, not just for the sake of tourism, but to keep the region's traditions alive.

Seeing China a second time in 2009, I kept asking myself how I would describe the country politically. It was obviously not the Communist regime I saw in 1979 when the shift toward private enterprise was only just beginning. Was the country Communist at all, or had it evolved to something else? Judging by burgeoning Shanghai and Beijing, China seemed as competitive, developed, and consumer-oriented as any Western country. Even in Guizhou, I got the feeling people were focused on acquiring things and living better lives. Thus, the real test of the Communist system, it seemed to me, has to do, not with economic issues, but with opportunities for political expression and opposition. Recalling the efforts made in the 1970s to impose the party line, I wondered how much repression people experienced in 2009 in their search for information and how free they were to express individual ideas.

As a starting point, when we used our laptops in Shanghai, it took a few minutes to go through censorship controls before the screen came to life. In the US, we often hear about Chinese control of the Internet. In a battle between the international powers of China and Google, I'd bet on a compromise over which both parties will declare victory. Does this mean that China has free expression? Of course not, but it does mean that control of information is no longer an infallible, or even a powerful, tool for controlling society.

Likewise, because we visited China just before the 20th anniversary of the government's 1989 assault on student protesters in Tiananmen Square, I wanted to know what the Chinese knew or felt about the event. I felt an urge to ask our tour guides but resisted in order not to discomfort them. I'm now sorry I didn't ask. Nonetheless, I read an article in the *New York Times* about the Tiananmen anniversary stating that a few former protesters and even military men were speaking out and an artist had mounted a photographic memorial, not the same as a government commemoration of Tiananmen, but noteworthy.

We were also in China just after the publication – not by the Chinese government – of "Prisoner of the State: the Secret Journal of Premier Zhao Zhiyang." This book was written by a former Premier of China from 1980 to 1987, who then became General Secretary of the Chinese Communist Party from 1987 to 1989 when Tiananmen occurred. Zhao Zhiyang criticized the government's decision to impose martial law and its failure to resolve the students' protests peacefully. My friends from Shanghai brought this controversial book back from Hong Kong, where it was published in both Chinese and English. Obviously, since the banned book had crossed to the mainland, it was surely making the rounds of the Chinese elite.

If Communism has waned, what does post-

Communism look like? Let's compare China with Asia's other great power, India. While Americans praise India for being a western-style, multi-party democracy with free elections, we criticize China for being a one-party system lacking democratic processes. I find that judgment superficial. India has multi-party elections, but the results are often determined by which party buys the most votes. China has only one party, but within that party there is definite competition, although not at the popular electoral level. In recent months, there has been open protest against the Chinese government by victims of natural disasters and against manufacturing enterprises by workers who feel underpaid and overworked.

As important as democratic process is the matter of who benefits from modernization. In India, the development process benefits the middle class and elites gaining from India's new role as a high tech giant. The rural poor, close to 600 million of them, have advanced little, comparable to populations in sub-Saharan Africa. In contrast, the Chinese economic revolution is more democratic than India's. While Chinese development has created millionaires and billionaires, it has also raised the standard of living dramatically for the rural poor. On the UN's 2009 Human Development Index, China ranked 92 out of 182, while India ranked 134. China's life expectancy was 72.9 years compared to 63.4 for India. Adult literacy was 93.3 percent for China, 66 percent for India. Finally, China's GDP per capita was $5383, while India's was $2753. China outperformed India despite having three hundred million more people.

Does that mean China is democratic? No, but it suggests China is creating a more egalitarian society that will – ultimately – push for more democracy. Yes, the Chinese environment is negatively affected by traffic, pollution and loss of open space, but, aware of the costs of modernization, the Chinese have invested heavily in clean energy, mass transit and decentralization. Yes, China has suffered from some terrible scandals based on fraud, but the willingness to expose and punish fraud is greater than ever.

While, after visiting India, I felt no urge to ever return, I feel eager to go back to China, a place where outsiders come to gape and also imitate.

Prayers for Nepal

As a young woman, I yearned to go to Nepal, hang out with hippies in Kathmandu, and test my physical prowess on a Himalayan trek. Why didn't I go? Because Nepal was halfway around the world, expensive to get to, and not the kind of place most of my friends wanted to visit. When I finally set out for Nepal in 2009, many years later, I quickly discovered Kathmandu is no longer a laid back hippie haven, and the kind of trekking trip I once envisioned was no longer possible due to age. Still, I had some great adventures.

My first challenge was getting there. I had enough miles to get a no-charge ticket on United Airlines and save $1800, but United insisted on sending me through China, stopping in Shanghai and then overnighting in Chengdu where no one at the airport spoke English. At 2 a.m. I ended up sharing a room in a hotel near the airport with a pleasant young Chinese woman who knew enough English to explain how the shower worked. At 7 a.m. my next plane took off for Kathmandu, or so I thought. Strangely, we landed in a dry, barren, mountainous area with no city in sight. It didn't look at all like the Nepal I'd imagined.

It turned out not to be Nepal at all, but Lhasa, Tibet, a one-hour stop on the way to Kathmandu that wasn't listed on my itinerary. When we finally took off again, I was in for the treat of my life. We flew parallel to the tops of the Himalayas between Nepal and China. That included the Everest range. The day was perfectly clear, and because the plane was at roughly the same altitude as the mountain tops, I felt as if I was near the Everest summit. The sights were stunning, and, of course, my camera was packed in my suitcase. I promised myself that, on the way home,

I would sit in a window seat between Kathmandu and Lhasa with my camera in my hand and would photograph the world's most breathtaking grandeur.

After my extraordinary flight from Lhasa, it was crushing to land in Kathmandu which, in recent years, has become an urban disaster. I'd been told the traffic was horrendous, but I'd previously been in Bangkok, Jakarta and Shanghai, all cities where the roads were disasters, so how bad could Kathmandu be? Worse. Not only were there an extraordinary number of cars, motorcycles, buses, trucks and bicycle-driven rickshaws, but the roads were also in terrible shape – two lane roads with broken shoulders, gigantic potholes in the middle of the only road out of town, cars broken down and abandoned in the middle of the street. Gridlock at all times of the day. A trip that would take a half hour as the crow flies took two hours. A logical solution, at least in the city center, would be to go by foot except that walking meant negotiating broken sidewalks or streets with no sidewalk at all. And forget maps – most streets, except the main avenues, lack names or street signs.

The nightmarish traffic was a huge frustration for the group of women I was traveling with. They gamely went on all our planned excursions, but not without many complaints. Along with the delays caused by the endless stream of vehicles were the black smoke and acrid fumes produced by decrepit buses and trucks as they inched down narrow streets. Snow-covered mountains, once visible from town, have disappeared in the smog. Pollution, combined with the altitude (6000 feet), produced headaches, bleary eyes, coughs and irritability.

Another tragic fact of life in Kathmandu was that nothing much worked. Electric power was periodic. At least the government posted the time of daily power cuts to warn the public. Most tourist amenities depended on unreliable generators, which, among other things, made for delayed meals in restaurants. Likewise, the fresh water of the Himalayas turned brown by the time it reached urban faucets. My group had been booked in a luxury hotel, but, despite its five star rating, it seemed rundown, in large part due to unreliable municipal services.

The only excursion I enjoyed in Kathmandu was to the medieval town of Bhaktapur, unfortunately outside of town so that getting there and back seemed interminable. Happily, Bhaktapur was traffic-free, its cobblestone streets closed to cars, although not motorbikes. The town had a string of ancient temples, monastery courtyards, monumental squares, and an artists' community boasting potters, weavers and woodcarvers. I was taken by the work of Tibetan refugees drawing intricate mandalas at an art school. Most of all, however, my pleasure came from observing people engaged in daily chores – pounding grain, collecting water at communal taps, hanging colorful dyed yarn out to dry, and sending their charming uniformed children off to school.

What made Kathmandu tolerable was the cheerful, patient and caring personalities of the Nepali people. While Nepalis expected to bargain when they sold their goods, they did so in a gentle manner as compared to, say, Turks or Indians. When Nepalis became friends, they quickly bestowed small gifts. I often wished I was carrying something to give in return. I discovered, amazingly, that, despite the traffic, Nepalis had polite driving habits. When I was stuck in an unmoving taxi for 20 minutes, I expected my driver to honk, swear or grumble, but he took our situation in stride. Even when driving on the torn up highways outside of town, drivers seemed to give way rather than pass other cars at the risk of a crash, although I did see a number of wrecked cars that had rolled off the pavement.

The chaos of Kathmandu can be explained in large part by the country's failure to maintain a functioning government. In recent years, Nepal has had to endure weak royal governance and an even weaker democratic system. Maoists organized an insurgent movement in the countryside that spread to the cities. Once the violent insurgency ended and the royalty was dismantled, Nepal was left with a power vacuum. At the time of my visit, many different political parties were trying to write a new constitution but they couldn't agree on anything except stopping decisions from being taken.

The Fund for Peace has defined "failed states" as countries experiencing state collapse. Nepal made the list only once in recent years, but I expect it will again since it lacks a viable development strategy and is reaching for modernity (cars and motorbikes, for example) without providing necessary infrastructure (roads). Nepal ranks at 142 out of 177 countries on the UN's 2009 Human Development Index. While its poverty and backwardness qualify it for international help, making change, even with foreign assistance, seems impossible in the face of political paralysis.

Outside of Kathmandu, visitors can still enjoy the delights of this Himalayan nirvana. Oddly enough, my first taste of beauty was not in the mountains but the jungle. My women's group flew from Kathmandu to Nepal's southern province, the Terai, where, roaming at the Royal Chitwan National Park, were one-horned rhinoceroses, deer, other small mammals, and on a rare occasion, tigers. I loved the jungle climate – warm, a bit humid, sunny -- perfect for lovers of tropical places.

Wildlife tourists couldn't possibly miss the trained elephants because they carried us into the park. From our elephant's back, we saw a rare mother rhino and her baby as well many exotic deer. From a tall wooden stand, I had no problem getting onto the elephant. Getting off was quite different. With the stiffness I acquired from sitting on the seat with three other people, I stumbled dismounting, bruised my legs and, black and blue, gave up wearing shorts for the rest of the trip.

I especially loved the jungle town outside the park. It ran alongside a gentle river where crocodiles seemed to pose for tourist cameras. There were many lovely small shops and cafes and the surrounding tropical foliage provided shelter for an array of exotic birds. I saw many of the plants I loved in Hawaii -- hibiscus, bougainvillea, wild ginger, bird of paradise. The tropical scenery made it hard to believe I was in a country with the highest mountains in the world!

We drove from Chitwan to Pokhara along a terrifying two-lane "highway" that had alluring glimpses of snowcapped mountains once we got to the foothills. Pokhara, once a small country town but now Nepal's second largest city, has grown rapidly as the center of mountain tourism. The best way to escape the hubbub of shops, street merchants, and cafes was to retreat to the Fish Tail Lodge, a deluxe hotel on Pokhara's lake reached by modest rope-drawn pontoons. The Annapurna range loomed in front, capped by Fish Tail, a sacred mountain closed to trekking.

Fish Tail Lodge had a wonderful tradition of waking new guests, if they wished, just before sunrise so they could photograph the mountains on the other side of the lake as they turned pink and amber in the dawn. On a clear day, the reflection of the mountains onto the lake created images that made me feel like Ansel Adams at work. Thoroughly happy at the hotel, which also had a lovely pool, I nonetheless did a bit of shopping in Pokhara for Tibetan beads and Nepali hand-made paper. Then

I quickly retreated to the hotel to sip a beer outside the restaurant and luxuriate in picture postcard views of Annapurna. Despite all my principles about not traveling in luxury, I wondered as I sipped my beer if I could get accustomed to the good life.

From Pokhara, most of our group went on a gentle trek, while three of us, who felt a bit physically "challenged," drove from Pokahara down the mountains to the hillside town of Bandipur, 1000 meters high up a curving mountain road, where we stayed overnight. Once a center for traders moving between India and Tibet, the village of Bandipur, with its centuries-old buildings preserved for visitors, had modernized with tourist amenities such as hostels and cafes. The view from Bandipur stretched across rolling hills and valleys of lush green rice paddies, which, in the early morning, were covered by wispy clouds and fog. Once again, the early morning photo opportunity was best of all. The Annapurna range, standing at 8000 plus meters, appeared, because we were also high, at eye level.

Although we regretted returning to Kathmandu's gridlock, we had an exciting program of meetings with non-governmental organizations (NGOs). There are over 1000 NGOs in Kathmandu, many with branches throughout the country. Nepal keeps functioning because of the work of its NGOs.

My first experience was with two women's organizations located in foothills 2-3 hours outside Kathmandu and established by World Neighbors, an American NGO. We first went to a women's health clinic, down a steep mountainside and set in a village surrounded by rich green rice paddies. The clinic served a large area of remote villages by providing basic gynecological and obstetric services to women who walk long distances to the clinic to receive care. I saw a woman, toothless when she smiled, who was being treated for uterine prolapse, a common problem resulting from either early childbirth or lack of rest after delivery. She was incredibly grateful to be given a vaginal ring, which cost little and made such a big difference!

We also traveled to a women's micro-loan project. Picture 40 very proud women sitting on the ground, all wearing red saris/salwar kameez and proudly sharing, one by one, their stories of buying and raising goats. The goats were raised by the cooperative, and, as they produced lambs, the offspring were given to individual women who contributed 5 rupees (a few US cents) every month to their fund. At that rate, it will take a long time to furnish goats to every family, but the women were determined to keep going. Naturally my women's group contributed enough to purchase one more goat.

One of Nepali women's serious problems is sex trafficking. Our group met with the founder of ABC/ Nepal which retrieves trafficked Nepali girls from brothels in India and provides them repatriation, care and rehabilitation. In Nepal, 7000 - 8000 girls are trafficked every year (many to Arab countries and India). Trafficking occurs because poor families are willing to sell their daughters for 10,000 rupees (about $140). ABC/Nepal locates trafficked girls by networking with Indian agencies, watching border traffic, and making occasional trips to Indian brothels known to purchase Nepali girls. Unfortunately, ABC/Nepal recovered only a small number of girls. If the government had a recovery program, a lot more would happen, but, as noted, the Nepali government today isn't even able to provide basic municipal services.

It was heartening to find one women's organization, the Association for Craft Producers (ACP), a business, not an NGO, that was self-staining and growing. ACP, a fair trade organization started in 1984, was run by a woman who provided work, primarily for women, in a large factory making all kinds of handicrafts -- clothing, bedding and housewares, toys, jewelry and delightful Christmas decorations – and carefully recycling its waste materials. ACP provided generous benefits to its employees, including scholarships for their children, and tried to maintain environmentally healthy workrooms, although some workers, refusing to acknowledge the dangers of chemical fumes, resisted putting on protective gear.

Perhaps the most original NGO I encountered was Empowering Women of Nepal (EWN), run by an all-women's trekking agency in Pokhara that has so far led over 200 treks. Lucky Chhetri's goal in starting EWN was to provide women opportunities in the trekking/tourism field by training them as guides. When our group asked how Nepali women could manage as porters, Lucky pointed to the huge loads of fabric or wood carried by women in the course of daily labor. EWN also provided child care for its women staff out on treks, and, having found many abandoned children in western Nepal, the organization established an orphanage for children next door to its Pokhara headquarters. Lucky's goal was to overcome cultural restraints against women while still respecting traditional ways such as wearing a salwar kameez, although not, of course, on treks!

In Kathmandu I visited TEWA, which means "support" in Nepalese, a philanthropic organization that raised money from individuals, corporate donors, and foundations to support "equitable justice and peace." When TEWA started, philanthropy was little known in Nepal and the Maoist insurgency made the social environment unstable. Nonetheless, TEWA had raised 1.6 million dollars and hoped to become a self-sustaining operation by renting out space in its lovely building containing offices, a cafeteria, meeting space, and an outdoor theater. TEWA donated 93 percent of its income to women's groups around the country because rural women were a promising investment. A sister organization, Nagarik Aawaz, was created by TEWA's founder to help youth displaced by the Maoist insurgency. The organization provided counseling, room and board, and peace education, and taught angry displaced youth the value of service by having them work in a Peace Kitchen for the poor.

Lastly, my favorite NGO, the Nepalese Youth Foundation (NYF) was started by Californian Olga Murray when she retired. Retired? First she built orphan homes in Kathmandu -- one for boys, then one for girls.

When word got out about these homes, desperate families were known to drop their children over the building's walls. To do something about malnutrition, Murray established Nutritional Rehabilitation Homes for hungry children and their mothers -- there are now 12 around Nepal. The children are referred by hospitals and mothers are asked to participate in the program so they can learn to cook and grow healthier foods than those found in the typical rural diet of rice and lentils. In a five-week stay at a nutritional home, most children go from skeletons to the average weight for their ages, and the mothers gain on average 12 pounds.

The NYF program that moved me the most was called Indentured Daughters. For years, NYF has bought back daughters in southwestern Terai who, at a young age, were indentured as servants to wealthy families. Typically, these girls were mistreated by their employers, often sexually abused. To stop the sale of young girls, NYF gave the girl's family a piglet or goat to make up for income lost from indenturing, brought the girl home and sent her to school. In one district, NYF has liberated 3000 girls. So many girls have been returned home that NYF has had to build additional classrooms. The best part was that the liberated girls have formed their own local organizations to publicize, through marches and street theater, the illegality and cruelty of indenturing.

The inspiration I got from the NGOs helping women and their families made up for the depression I felt witnessing Nepal's dysfunctional development. While I went to Nepal to see the magnificence of nature, I came home remembering, more than anything, the ways in which humanitarians, Nepalis and foreigners, were able to move mountains of another kind.

Our last day in Nepal, our group visited the country's most important Hindu shrine on the bank of the Bagmati River. In the cremation ghats corpses wrapped in white cloth were burned, the ashy remains thrown into the sacred river. While I respect the Hindu practice of cremation, it upset me to see children swimming in the polluted water just a small way downstream.

At the enormous Buddhist Bodnath Stupa sitting on top of a multi-level pedestal, hordes of Buddhist pilgrims, many of them Tibetan refugees, walked, chanting, clockwise around the base. Mixed in were tourists who began circling but soon dropped out in order to shop in the exhausting array of stalls selling Tibetan goods. We escaped the crowd by climbing three flights to an open air tearoom on the terrace of one of the buildings. From up high, the pilgrims and tourists seemed like a swarm of bees circling a hive. It was a rare day when the sky was less polluted and we could actually see snowy mountains in the distance. Our group ended the day with dinner in a traditional Nepali restaurant. After two weeks of Nepali food, I felt that if I never ate *dal* again, I would have no regrets.

I departed early the next morning. I had my camera in my carry-on bag and was delighted the day was clear and bright. On my flight to Lhasa, I sat by the window on the Everest side of the plane and started snapping pictures as soon as the Himalayas came into view. While I took many photos, none captured the exhilaration I felt when I saw those mountains for the first time and sensed that, at last, I had made it to the top of the world.

I doubt I will ever again visit Nepal, but I will say prayers for the country's future. While stunned by nature's performance, whether in the incomparable Himalayas or tropical jungle, I was also benumbed by uncontrolled urban growth. I will pray for a political resolution that allows Nepal to establish a functioning government and respond to the country's chaotic urbanization process while preserving its natural uniqueness.

I will have to say a lot of prayers.

PART IV

NEW WAYS TO TRAVEL

Christmas with Sinterklaas

Most of what I remember from my first visit to Amsterdam* is the cold. I went to the Netherlands in February, 1983, with an Israeli friend who was attending a conference. While I had packed sweaters, gloves, boots and a wool hat, I shivered most of the time. To cheer myself as I trudged through wet, dirty snow, I conjured up crisp, clear days and rosy-cheeked people ice-skating on the canals. Those images didn't change reality – the weather stayed rainy, the ground, slushy, and the sky, the color of lead. The cold made me think my bones were cracking.

So why, in 2009, would I leave California in wintertime to go back to Amsterdam? I had one compelling reason

– to visit Katerina, who had been studying and working in Amsterdam for several years. I hadn't seen my Greek god-daughter for eighteen months, and Jim hadn't seen her for even longer. I had little idea what her Dutch life was like and I had never met Darius, her Lithuanian boyfriend.

The trip came about in a touching way. In November, as Jim and I finished dinner at home in Santa Rosa, I gazed at the few sips of wine left in my glass and confided I was dreading Christmas. It wasn't the first time I'd felt that way. At Christmas, Jim and I miss family celebrations because his children are on the East Coast and usually spend holidays with family members who live closer to them. Even though our California friends invite us to join them, I long for a family occasion of my own. Christmas without your own family isn't much of a holiday.

When Jim suggested we go somewhere to "escape," I appreciated his thought but couldn't come up with any place enticing. I couldn't imagine traveling in winter, unless going somewhere to escape the cold, someplace like Hawaii, Mexico or the Caribbean. Those places were already booked and incredibly expensive at that time of year.

"So what should we do?" he asked.

Although in a holiday funk, I had one magical idea – to be with the young person I considered my own surrogate child. "This is crazy," I said, "but if we go anywhere, I'd like to be with Katerina."

"Go to Amsterdam? In winter?" Jim said in surprise. "Are you serious?"

"She's my god-daughter, our god-daughter, and we haven't seen her in so long."

Jim's wrinkled his eyebrows, then grinned. "Well, you'd better start looking for tickets."

I was ecstatic. First I emailed Katerina to make sure she would be in Amsterdam at Christmastime. When I presented my idea of a visit, she answered immediately with a short email, saying, "Book, book, book." The only reasonable tickets I could "book" had us flying to Amsterdam on Christmas Day when no one else wants to be in the air. That didn't bother me. I didn't mind eating a tasteless airline Christmas dinner or arriving after Christmas on December 26. I just wanted to see Katerina.

I rushed out to buy a *Lonely Planet Guidebook*. The book's cover depicted everyone's fantasy of Holland – feet in wooden clogs and big rounds of Gouda cheese. I had always thought wooden shoes were related to Holland's below-sea level topography, but discovered that clogs or *klompen* are worn throughout northern Europe. Today most people wear plastic clogs and bring out wooden ones only for gardening. Other traditional photos of Holland showed windmills, canals and tulips, but, beyond the kitsch, I knew Holland had a rich history, political and cultural life. In a week's visit, I wouldn't get to do much but I planned to get a taste of all of those when I wasn't hanging out with Katerina.

I studied the guidebook's map of Amsterdam. It was daunting, especially since I knew not one word of Dutch although I figured out that *gracht* meant canal. I emailed Katerina to ask what section of the city she lived in and she sent back a Google map. Thank heavens for Google. Once I figured out her area, I was able to pick out some hotels that were nearby. I checked out web sites and chose a hotel that advertised three-star quality at two-star prices. I hoped it would live up to its reputation.

I was glad the hotel didn't serve breakfast since *Lonely Planet* described a typical Dutch breakfast as "filling yet unexciting – a few slices of bread accompanied by jam, cheese and a boiled egg." It would be far preferable to hit one of the 1000 cafes in Amsterdam or a *broodjeszaken* (sandwich shop). I fantasized ordering a plate of cheeses. Based on the discovery of ancient pots that separated curds from whey, cheese has been made in the area since prehistoric times. Smoky cheese, sour cheese, Gouda, Edam, the thought was divine, even for breakfast.

I had conflicting impressions of Dutch character. I envisioned people who were calm, reserved and resourceful. After all, they had reclaimed much of their country from land under water and, with huge dikes, had kept the roiling North Sea at bay. The notion of a "Dutch treat" made me think of the Dutch as parsimonious, if not stingy. At the same time, the Dutch had progressive social policy with generous benefits. I applauded their liberal positions on drugs, prostitution, gay marriage and euthanasia. How could people who were personally reserved also be so accepting of unconventional social behavior?

A website on Dutch culture tried to explain this anomaly, arguing that, above everything, the Dutch are pragmatic. On the issue of drugs, for example, the website maintained:

> A Dutch person would think: If soft drugs were forbidden, then their use and traffic would go underground and no one could legally control it any further. Furthermore, the prices would go up, forcing some users into criminal behavior sooner rather than later.

So the Dutch legalized mild drugs such as marijuana and hashish. That made perfect sense to me. If only the U.S. were so pragmatic instead of pretending marijuana is used only for medicinal purposes.

Although the U.S. hasn't followed Holland's marijuana laws, at least it adopted Santa Claus from Sinterklaas, the Christmas character introduced by Dutch settlers when they colonized New York's Hudson Valley. Sinterklaas, here we come.

The best part of arriving in Amsterdam was being met at the airport by Katerina, who was holding a big bunch of roses and was accompanied by her partner Darius. I hadn't been expecting them, but knowing Katerina's loving nature, I wasn't surprised they were there. Even in the cold north of Europe, Katerina looked Mediterranean with her shining dark brown eyes and long, wavy dark hair. Darius, tall, well-groomed, and ruddy-cheeked, had the broad cheekbones and wide face common to people from the Baltics. I could see from their togetherness they were a happy couple, and that made me happy.

Katerina and Darius shepherded us onto an airport train to Central Station and then onto trams to our hotel. I'm not sure we could have managed getting our suitcases, loaded with gifts, onto the various trains but strong and helpful Darius was there to carry both bags.

Our hotel was located in an old-style building right next to a tram stop. "Location" is the best thing I can say about the hotel. We entered from the street into a stairwell no more than a yard wide that stank of cigarettes and had extremely steep, winding steps going up a flight to the reception. As soon as we got to the reception desk, I was ready to change hotels except that it was a very busy Christmas week and I feared we would not find anything else. And, since I'd booked online, the hotel already had my credit card number.

I asked to see the room, and we climbed another steep flight of stairs. At least our room was large, with tall windows, and non-smoking. Its cheap, ugly furniture was rescued only by Katerina's red and yellow roses. We had a kind of mock Christmas as Jim and I played Mr. and Mrs. Sinterklaas and unloaded from our suitcases all the cosmetics, creams, and clothing we had brought for Katerina and Darius. Then, having experienced a three-hour airport delay in San Francisco and ten hours in the air, we were ready to collapse on our creaky bed. We hoped things would look better in the morning. What morning? At three a.m., we were woken by a pair of young women returning to the room next door after a night of partying. They shouted, laughed uproariously, and refused to acknowledge our angry knocks on the wall.

The next day, after an expensive, Euro-priced, breakfast in a café, Jim and I began our round of museums. We made our visits without Katerina, who had work to do during the day, and without Darius, who was studying for exams. The neighborhood Jim and I were staying in, once the Jewish quarter of town, had many museums within walking distance. Bundled up in long underwear, we found the weather decent enough to stroll around.

Amsterdam had an astounding number of major and minor museums, which not only featured art but also history, trades, foreign affairs, and crafts. We began with the stately, newly established Hermitage Museum, an annex of the grand and glorious Hermitage in Saint

Petersburg. The opening exhibit, "Palace and Protocol," an introduction to the nineteenth century Russian Court, contained walls of royal portraits and displays of luxurious gowns, jewels and men's formal wear. I would have preferred to see Hermitage art works but, clearly, Dutch museum-goers were fascinated by displays of tsarist excess.

That afternoon, we stopped in to see Verzetsmuseum, a small museum in our neighborhood that featured the Dutch Resistance in World War II. Foreigners, most of whom know the diary of Anne Frank, think of the Dutch as brave resisters. On my first visit to Amsterdam, I'd seen her hideout and the museum dedicated to her book. This time, I was interested in getting additional perspectives about the Dutch role in the war.

Perhaps contrary to the Resistance Museum's intent, the exhibit left me with a strong impression that the prevailing Dutch attitude had <u>not</u> been to resist but to get along with the German invaders and return, as quickly as possible, to business as usual. Holland's surrender to the Germans came four days after the invasion, and once Germany had pushed on to Belgium and France, the Dutch resumed their lives, free of fighting. Of course, there was some Dutch resistance to the Nazis – strikes, a few protests over discrimination against Jews, organizations that helped Jews hide – but, for the most part, the Dutch seemed to find the Jewish presence in Holland a nuisance. While 25,000 Jews were, like the Frank family, able to hide, 107,000 were taken to death camps and only 5000 returned.

My initial impression was reinforced the next day when I visited the Jewish Historical Museum in a restored synagogue. The World War II exhibit explained that a few fortunate Jews were able, at a cost of about 100 guilders a month, to purchase ration cards, false identification papers and transport out of Holland. The rest had to scramble on their own. After the war, Dutch Jews, according to the Museum Guide, again had an exceedingly difficult time:

The government did not take any measures to address

the specific problems of the Jewish population, arguing that they did not wish to discriminate as the German occupying forces had done. The decades following 1945 witnessed a bitter struggle for redress. The Dutch public was coping with its own poverty and distress and had little interest in or sympathy for the plight of the survivors.

Helping Jewish victims was a form of discrimination? That's a far less appealing picture of Dutch attitudes than the Anne Frank story.

My last museum visit was to the world-famous Van Gogh Museum. The paintings were fabulous – more than 200 of Van Gogh's works, many well-known masterpieces and numerous small works and self-portraits. Van Gogh's short life was remarkable. He started to paint at 27, essentially self-taught, and despite trying economic straits, was prolific for ten years until he took his life in 1890 at age 37.

I have always felt Van Gogh, alone and lonely, projected his emotional life and moods directly onto his paintings, communicating the ecstasy of beauty and the despair of everyday existence. His museum failed to capture the man or the mental illness that drove him. The biographical material was dry and restrained, the paintings were hung in pedestrian chronological order. Van Gogh deserved a more creative presentation than he received in his museum. I would have appreciated discussions of his personality, lifestyle and mental illness and contrasts from his times of joy with his periods of his inner turmoil. Unfortunately, the museum did none of that. No wonder Van Gogh escaped gloomy Holland for a more expressive place like France.

Beyond museums, I was extremely interested in learning about Muslim life in Holland. I knew thousands of Turks had come to Holland in the 1960s and 1970s as *gastbeiters*, guest workers. I was not aware of the large presence of Moroccans until 2004 when 26-year-old Mohammed Bouveri first shot, then stabbed to death film-maker Theo Van Gogh, a descendant of the painter, in reaction to his film "Submission," a critique of women's lives under Islam. Bouveri, an educated and employed Dutch citizen, had fallen under the influence of a radical Syrian cleric promoting a holy war against the west.

Bouveri was an exception, however. Few of the 320,000 Turks and 280,000 Muslims in Holland are radical Islamists. Most are second or third generation immigrants whose families arrived when the Dutch needed workers for their expanding economy. Although permission to bring in workers ended officially in 1973, Muslim immigration continued as workers brought their families to Holland under liberal reunification laws. Today, when immigrants from the Middle East are included, there are 850,000 Muslims in Holland or five percent of the population.

The Dutch have had serious problems integrating Muslims into society. Admittedly, Muslims in small numbers have been elected to Parliament or appointed to high government positions. Yet, while I saw a number of darker-skinned people on public transport, in service jobs, or working as tram drivers or museum guards, I never saw interpersonal interactions between the white population and Muslims. In my god-daughter's lower income neighborhood, a short distance by tram from the center of town, there were many Turkish people and shops. Katerina observed that interpersonal relations occurred over business transactions and little else. The failure of integration is based in large part on economics. The Dutch no longer have enough jobs for second and third generation Muslim residents. Unemployed Muslim youth reportedly spend much time plugged into media-based violent rhetoric either on television or the Web. At the same time, many Dutch have reacted negatively to the immigrants' presence in Holland, especially after the Van Gogh killing. In 2008-2009, they tightened immigration laws to require that immigrants pass – in their home country – a test of their Dutch. To cut down on brides immigrating from other countries, the Dutch have required Muslim grooms to be at least 21 and have an income 120% of the minimum wage.

Even if these restrictions cut down on new immigration,

problems of assimilation will remain. Like other northern Europeans, the Dutch face immigrant frustration at the same time that militancy is proliferating. In truth, the only things from a Muslim country – Turkey – the Dutch ever fully embraced were tulips. When I thought about the problem of integrating Muslims, it reminded me of the Dutch relations, in an earlier period, with Jews. Evidently, small, homogeneous countries like the Netherlands have a hard time coping with outsiders.

A visit to Amsterdam has to include some tourist highlights and ours was a canal cruise. It had snowed the night before and canal buildings were framed in glistening white. Amsterdam has 100 canals which are necessary for survival since at high tide the city is only a yard and a half above sea level. The fisher folk who founded the city in 1275 also understood that housing had to be built on stilts. By the 17th century, the canals were shaped to form concentric circles around the city center. In that period, Amsterdam gained considerable wealth from its role in world trade. Residences were built by wealthy merchants, financiers, professionals and craftsmen.

Since Amsterdam was a small city, narrow houses – about 30 feet wide -- were constructed with long barely passable stairs inside. In order to bring furniture into the house, rooftop pulleys attached to furniture hooks were used. Even today, moving involves hoisting furniture or goods up the outside of the building using a hook extending from the top gable. Handsome from the outside, Amsterdam architecture inside is practical, if not particularly comfortable.

Another cultural highlight was an evening of music in the famous concert hall, the Concertgebouw. Katerina planned for the four of us to attend a performance in the *grote zaal,* great hall, that housed a three-story high organ. Beforehand, we had a lovely dinner of tea sandwiches and wine in the hall's restaurant, then heard an Edif Piaf concert by a fantastic Dutch singer. The hall, however, was the real star of the evening – a neo-classical wonder with acoustics that were engineered in 1888 and remain renowned all over the world. Given the small number of microphones above the stage, I was deeply impressed by the sound.

A last aspect of Amsterdam tourism to mention are the famous coffee houses where customers consume coffee and smoke marijuana. Having heard much about these "evil" dens, I was eager to visit one. Because Jim didn't approve, I snuck away with Katerina . The selection of marijuana or hashish cigarettes for purchase was so wide I would have had no idea where to start. Fortunately, I had Katerina to guide us. Ironically, one thing not allowed in the coffee houses is tobacco because of a no smoking ban in restaurants and cafes. When we mixed our marijuana with tobacco, we did so very discreetly. The coffee house was pleasant – soft music, subdued customers, no cigarette smoke in the air and no pressure to finish whatever you ordered and make room for other customers.

I was happy to have some time alone with Katerina, and we discussed her family news, her future move to England, and her hopes to find a job there in psychology.

She came to Holland to get a master's degree in health psychology at the University of Leiden but, because her Dutch was limited, after graduation she ended up working in the English-speaking offices of international shoe companies. She was waiting for Darius to get his B.S. in mathematical economics and then, as European Union citizens, they can go together to England. We all dreamed of having them come to the U.S., but that was almost impossible given U.S. visa restrictions.

One evening, the four of us engaged in an activity unique to Holland – drinking *jenever*, the Dutch national drink. *Jenever*, brewed from juniper berries, is the favorite alcoholic beverage in the country. We went to a noisy, smoky bar crammed with laughing young people near the famous Dam Square. We pushed to the counter to get small, liqueur-looking, glasses filled to the brim with a pale brown liquid. We then had to push our way back to the street to sit on benches in the alley and sip away. Even though it was frigid outdoors, we didn't feel it. *Jenever*, known as Dutch gin, was raw and bitter, undoubtedly an acquired taste that definitely took away the cold.

Our best evenings were spent with Katerina and Darius in their small but cheerful apartment, reached by climbing five flights of narrow stairs. Katerina cooked us Greek food, Darius served and cleared dishe,s and we brought the wine. We were happy to get to know Darius. I especially enjoyed how he and Jim bonded discussing their common interest in math. I asked Katerina and Darius how they felt living among the Dutch whom I found, as expected, reserved and distant. They agreed, describing the Dutch as rule-bound and impersonal. I pointed out the Dutch have a mellow time smoking marijuana in a coffee house or downing a glass of *jenever* after work. Katerina was convinced their inner joy had to be ignited with an external stimulant. I warned her she would never find northern Europeans that behaved like Greeks.

For me, Amsterdam was a fine place to visit, but I wouldn't want to live there. Like Van Gogh, I'd feel freer and more inspired by France. And, while I shivered less than during my first visit, the next time I visit Holland, it will not be when the snow is falling but when the tulips are in bloom.

Still, my trip to Amsterdam accomplished what my heart needed. I was able to celebrate the holiday season with young people who, without any blood ties, felt like my family. That is the best way for me to cope with Christmas blues – to travel to my loved ones -- even if it's in a frigid place. I hope we'll be together for other holiday seasons. Who knows? Maybe next year in California.

Searching for Mexico in San Miguel

Over my many years of traveling, I have avoided expat communities in the same way I've avoided the flu – by staying far away. Although I have been an expatriate, a foreigner living overseas, and have socialized with other expats, I have never traveled to an "expatriate community" for a holiday. At least not until 2010 when I went for a short winter vacation to San Miguel de Allende, an expat community in the highlands of central Mexico.

It had been a cool and rainy winter at home in Santa Rosa and I desperately wanted some sun. I persuaded my college roommate, Sherry, who lives in Chicago and was even more eager for sun than I, to take a short vacation south of the border. I suggested Belize or a Mexican beach to which Sherry replied, "Please, no beaches." Then, I came up with San Miguel. Sherry was intrigued, having heard about the town from friends and anticipating its consistently dry, spring weather.

I was also intrigued. Californian friends were wildly enthusiastic about San Miguel and kept going back. An artist friend from Santa Rosa owned a house outside San Miguel and often brought her students there for excursions. And I had an acquaintance, Patrice, who had settled in San Miguel ten years earlier after closing her women's bookstore in Berkeley. I emailed her to ask about apartment rentals or hotels, and she happily offered to rent her own house since she could use the time away to visit Mexico City. She sent me a glowing description of her home and Sherry and I agreed it sounded delightful. We arranged our visit for the first two weeks of February. Sherry later asked how I felt about having her husband Tom along for a week. (We would be a threesome since Jim had no interest in travel to Mexico.) I was pleased to have a charming, thoughtful and engaging male like Tom along for the first half of the trip. I packed up my spring clothes, threw in a couple of sweaters, just in case, and geared up for expat life.

The drive from the international airport in Leon to San Miguel, about 90 minutes, passed through a high desert-like landscape with scattered clumps of leafy trees and stands of prickly pear cactus dotting the beige earth – the kind of scenery I associated with 1950s westerns. When, from a distance, I caught sight of San Miguel, its pink, tan, ochre, blood red and umber buildings rising up semi-circular hillsides, I was surprised such a large habitation existed in, what seemed to me, the middle of nowhere.

San Miguel de Allende, in the state of Guanajuato, was a city of about 150,000 people. Expats made up only about 10 percent of the entire city, but because they were concentrated in homes and apartments around the historic center, they seemed more numerous than they were. In addition, *el centro* was the tourist heart and contained the bulk of fine hotels, restaurants and shops, like the foreigners' hole in a Mexican doughnut.

My friend Patrice's house was not in *el centro* but in a predominantly Mexican neighborhood in the northwest part of town. I was glad about that since I enjoyed seeing locals on the streets, kids playing on the sidewalks, and small *tiendas* (shops) selling groceries, beer, and household items. I laughed at the local method of garbage collection with garbage trucks announcing their presence by striking a large triangle over and over, at which point residents ran out of their houses with their brimming plastic bags. A few blocks from Patrice's house was a fine taco restaurant, open only in the late afternoon and evening. Even though we arrived in early afternoon before they opened, they served us a scrumptious lunch of tacos filled with shrimp, shredded pork and chicken, simply because we were there.

San Miguel's celebrated history went back to the sixteenth century when a nobleman, Ignacio Allende, led a revolt against Spanish colonialists. In the twentieth century, the town evolved into an artists' community, when in the late 1930s a Peruvian, together with an American, opened a school for artists in an abandoned convent. After a rocky beginning, the Escuela Universitaria de Bellas Artes took off after World War II, in part because U.S. veterans were able to attend with support from the GI Bill. The school became the Instituto Allende and attracted some well-known Mexican artists, such as Siqueiros, as instructors. Today, the Instituto, a grand old building with a lovely courtyard and a historic mural running the length of a wall, provides art and language classes, small galleries, a café and restaurant.

Artists from North America, Mexico and Europe have flocked to San Miguel. Art galleries were everywhere. I chatted with one American painter and craftsperson who, inspired by her night-time dreams, had started art work as a second career and already had a gallery at the Instituto. She told me the artists' community prided itself on being able to have frequent exhibits and on working in a community of peers who appreciated each other's work.

Most of the professional work I saw had certain commonalities – bright colors, whimsical figures and animals, spiritual symbols. In contrast, the artwork for tourists tended to concentrate on certain themes: skulls and skeletons representing Dia de los Muertos; portraits of Our Lady of Guadalupe in her robes; and Frida Kahlo's portrait and copies of her paintings. Diego Rivera, Frida's husband, *muertos* yet no doubt envious, is probably turning over in his grave.

San Miguel was a bevy of cobblestone streets lined with stucco buildings painted in earth tones, decorated with brightly colored doors and house numbers, and bearing intricate wrought iron railings. The buildings housed shops, cafes, restaurants, inns and homes, many of which also lined the small alleys between the streets. Most of the shops carried higher priced clothing and home decor. For bargains, visitors went to the Mercado de Artesianas, also in the center, where local people had stalls full of ceramics, jewelry, scarves, small paintings and trinkets. The Mercado catered to tourists while the residential expats tended to shop in the better stores.

The center of the downtown was *El Jardin*, the Garden, a plaza with dark green topiary trees in the middle and arcades of shops on three sides. On the fourth side stood San Miguel's best known feature, *La Parroquia,* a four story Gothic cathedral with rose-colored spires that could be seen from anywhere in town. The cathedral inside had silver decorative work, crystal chandeliers, and collections of *milagros,* tiny symbols of body parts and figures of males and females left by those wishing for the miracles of healing or romance.

Across a side street from the cathedral was Ignacio Allende's grand home, which has been turned into a historical museum. Allende's life and rebellious exploits, for which he was ultimately executed, were presented on the ground floor. On the second floor, elegant family rooms were decorated in the styles of the16[th] and 17th centuries and depicted the lives of wealthy residents, a mix of Spanish and Mexican. Wandering around *El Centro* was a delight, and San Miguel was a walking town, although it also benefitted from fleets of inexpensive roving taxis and modern buses.

One way to see some of the foreigners' beautiful homes was to join a Sunday house tour sponsored by La Biblioteca (the Library). Local buses took visitors to private homes in the countryside or around town. On my tour, I saw an extraordinary home in Atotonilco on the outskirts of San Miguel that was once part of a hacienda. Reconstructed by a male couple, it had front walls and rooms dating back to the 1750s, and modern new rooms (with enormous terrazzo stone bathrooms) that combined antique furniture with modern art. I especially loved the property's grounds with swimming pool, fish pond and Japanese tea house. One of the owners, an American with a gray crew cut and several silver earrings, told me the property would go on sale the following year. I briefly fantasized about living in such a place but could never have afforded it.

The second home on the tour was down a small alley, *callejon*, in the heart of *el centro*. It featured two wings with high, open spaces for hanging paintings and positioning sculpture done by the owners. Much of the house decor was capricious, such as a tile snake that wound through a bathroom to end in a shower. To add to the art, the American owners had covered the house and terraces with bright-colored plants and flowers, and thoughtfully arranged for guitar players to play Spanish duets throughout the tour.

Restaurants in San Miguel ranged from inexpensive Mexican restaurants, which were great for lunches and specialized in dishes like tortilla soup and chile rellenos, to relatively expensive foreign restaurants for dinner that offered American, European and Asian cuisines. For dinner, I especially enjoyed Cajun blackened fish in one restaurant and Italian scallopini with porcini mushrooms in another. What made the food especially delicious was a variety of local beers at lunch and a margarita or two at dinner. We all felt a little gastronomic excess at night was justified by the long, invigorating walks we took during the day.

Not only did we soak up the town, we also soaked in it. Over eight days, we had an extraordinary siege of bad weather. It rained for four days – sometimes, torrents, other times, steady rain. A drizzle felt like a beautiful day. The rains swelled the stream through the middle of town. Normally, it percolated over rocks in the stream bed but, after torrents, the water rose so high the police closed the bridges. Along with a few local people I had to sneak on foot across a bridge, with a policeman yelling at us, to reach my side of town. My friend Patrice later told me the month of February got 23 inches of rain when normally it got one quarter inch.

What made the rain even worse was the cold in our house. Apparently, local habitations did not have heating systems, although most foreigners and hotels had put in heat or provided space heaters. Our charming, colorful, and exquisitely decorated home had neither. When home, we three visitors huddled around a weak gas fireplace and tried to raise the temperature a few degrees in our bedrooms by sharing a single, minuscule portable heater. We thought of going out to buy space heaters, but were told the supply in the stores had been exhausted. The temperature inside the house went from fifty to, at best, sixty degrees and forced us to sleep in several layers of clothing and go to the bathroom in our coats. Naturally, we considered moving to a hotel, but none of us wanted to pay for a second room after we had already paid for the house. Our ultimate response to the rain and cold was to cut short our visit by a week.

I envied the fact that my friends on the trip were a couple and could share body heat in their king size bed. I discovered that traveling with another couple was different from what I expected. While my friends were wonderfully thoughtful and inclusive, married folks interact in ways that inevitably leave out the single companion. As one example, my friends always prepared their own breakfast together without including me. Most likely, I would have preferred my own breakfast menu, but I wanted to be asked.

One evening as we huddled around the gas fire, I mentioned to Sherry and Tom my feeling about being the third wheel.

"I'm having a great time with you two," I said, "but I can't help feeling at times like I'm the odd one out."

"Oh, dear," Sherry said. "We don't ever want you to feel that way. Can you tell me when we might have excluded you?"

"Oh, you never excluded me. It's just that communication between husband and wife is inevitably more 'connected'. That's just a feature of a couple and an 'extra' traveling together."

Truly, in no way did I blame my friends. If our positions had been reversed, I'm sure I would have behaved the same way with my own husband. What I did learn, however, was that traveling as a "couple plus one" didn't work well for me. Since being with dear friends like Sherry and Tom was undoubtedly the best case scenario, I doubt

I will travel with a couple again. I really missed being partnered and was eager to get home to Jim.

Most people go to San Miguel for vacations, classes, and artistic endeavors. In contrast, I wanted to learn something about my passion in life – non-governmental organizations (NGOs) that serve women and children. Through my hostess, I was introduced to several organizations in San Miguel that promote girls' education and aid dependent groups in the Mexican population such as the ill or aged.

Mujeres en Cambio was a philanthropic effort to help girls in the *campo,* countryside, finish school and, in a few cases, attend college. Girls in the *campo* were more likely than city girls to drop out of middle or high school because of the expense. While public education was free through sixth grade, middle school and high school were costly for the indigent, especially the $40 per semester tuition that must be paid up front. Families in the *campo* were desperately poor, often making only $5 per day, and lacked funds to pay for fees, purchase books and transportation, and buy uniforms and shoes. Through Mujeres en Cambio, girls received $25 per month, and college students, $1000 per year. To qualify for the program, girls were closely monitored. They had to attend school regularly and maintain a grade point average of 8 out of 10.

Begun in 1995, Mujeres en Cambio grew from supporting 8 girls to 150 girls today, and 43 young women in university. The girls, from 8 small communities, were chosen by their teachers and principals. The organization's funds were raised through individual contributions and ten charity luncheons held each year in San Miguel where the food was prepared by expat volunteers.

What impressed me most was the commitment of Mujeres en Cambio to the countryside. While working people in San Miguel are exposed to new opportunities in the tourist sector, *campesinos* are stuck in farming, mostly growing beans, in a rugged agricultural environment. The state of Guanajuato surrounding San Miguel is one of the poorest in Mexico. For a girl, education makes all the difference between a life on a struggling farm and obtaining a secure clerical or service job in a city. Unlike other expat volunteer activities in San Miguel – such as working on the Library which was mostly used by expats – Mujeres en Cambio reached those at the bottom in terms of both poverty and gender.

I also encountered a local foundation established by an American expat in his will as his legacy to San Miguel. The foundation contributed to several causes: students trying to go to university, a school for the deaf and mute, midwifery training for girls, and instruction for *campesinos* on producing organic and sustainable goods. The woman foundation director was at first hesitant to speak with me, believing, I think, that I was an expat assessing her work. Once I established that I was researching NGOs and was somewhat bewildered by San Miguel's expat character, she opened up. She was not optimistic about the long-term survival of her foundation. Having made initial monetary contributions, she was already low on funds and was having difficulty raising more money. She felt most expats were uninterested in grass roots activities, wanting instead to take on visible do-gooder projects that were "bandaids" with no impact on "transforming the community."

Apparently, her expat board was reluctant to promote Mexicans as change-makers. I asked about adding Mexicans to her board. That would be a problem, she explained, and gave as an example the newly elected woman mayor of San Miguel who had campaigned on "San Miguel for the San Miguelenses" and, consequently, was unpopular with some expats. The director doubted San Miguel would ever be a place where foreigners would foster social change since they liked the town the way it was.

She commented further on the overall impact of the expat community, noting that resident foreigners drove up the cost of many things, especially housing. Most local people had to move to the edge of town. She also objected to the social environment, pointing out that most expats spoke little Spanish except daily greetings and preferred workers who spoke some English. She observed that locals, when hired by foreigners, performed desired tasks but never learned creative ideas behind them. For example, a foreigner running a homemade clothing shop used locals as seamstresses but never taught them about design. As she put it, "real development is not about telling people what to do."

To outsiders, expats in San Miguel had brought about fine results – a beautifully restored city, excellent tourist facilities, an active cultural life of classes, exhibits, a library, theater group, house tours. The town was thriving, but who benefitted? Perhaps a few of the local people in the area, but certainly not a large proportion of them. Every additional peso earned by a local had to be weighed against the significantly higher cost of living brought by foreigners.

I asked a Mexican shop owner, wearing her own vivid homemade clothes and bead jewelry, how she felt about the expat presence. She replied that foreigners had definitely changed the nature of town, "still, they are good for business." She missed the village that San Miguel had once been and was sorry her children would never know what it was like to live there without consumerism and "dependence on Americans."

I began to see "expatriatism" as a contemporary form of colonialism. While expats are not trying to conquer Mexico or exploit the land for minerals, most are living in ways that make life better for themselves but not necessarily for others. They have settled in Mexico because it is warm, despite my patch of bad weather, and relatively inexpensive for a foreign retiree's wallet. And it is close to the U.S. You can easily drive there from Texas (a lot of the expats are Texans) and fly from anywhere else in the U.S., usually via Houston. The town is relatively safe – no signs yet of drug cartels. And perhaps most important, it is familiar, a quasi-American culture from pilates classes to cajun restaurants to Starbucks. It's home away from home with no need to adapt to a foreign culture. As my traveling companions put it, we were "only halfway in a foreign land."

"Home away from home" is the reason I will not return to San Miguel and will avoid, as much as possible, other expat communities. Hearing English much of the time, eating California nouvelle cuisine, making long distance phone calls on American Internet lines – all these things made me long for a truly foreign vacation.

The word "expatriate" comes from Latin and means "out of country" or, according to Webster's, "to leave one's native country." I am all for expatriates who have made a decision to leave home and immerse themselves in new communities. I object to expat locations like San Miguel where Americans go to encounter people just like themselves and to replicate their home culture. And San Miguel is not alone. There are other similar expat communities in Europe, Hong Kong, even Shanghai. My objection is not with any individual place but with the notion of trying to recreate home when you are abroad. I ask myself why people travel to a foreign country where the American experience keeps intruding and eroding the native environment.

Perhaps San Miguel will always be located in Mexico, but I fear it may some day cease, in any real way, being Mexican.

The Costs of Volunteering

Volunteer at an NGO overseas? That sounded like an ideal way for an inveterate do-gooder like me to travel. Jim agreed a volunteer experience with International Helpers would be just the thing – not for him, but for me. I went to the I-Helpers website and clicked on "destinations." The second one on the list clicked in my brain – the South Pacific. While Jim and I had lived in Hawaii for six years, I'd never been anywhere else in the Pacific and was dying to explore other islands, snorkel among dazzling colored fish, and bake in the brilliant sun. I quickly signed up for a two-week trip.

The destination turned out to be the Cook Islands, a

place I had to look up on the map. The fifteen Cook Islands are small and far-flung, dotting the ocean between New Zealand and Tahiti. The more populated southern group sits hundreds of miles away from the barely populated northern group which is quite cut off from development. Even in the southern group island-hopping by plane or boat is time-consuming, infrequent and expensive. I-Helpers held its program on Rarotonga, the main southern island, which, happily, I could reach directly from Los Angeles on Air New Zealand's once-a-week flight.

As the day of my departure approached, I gathered all my tropical vacation necessities, although it would be winter below the Equator with cooler temperatures and ocean water than usual. At the bottom of my suitcase went suntan lotion, bathing suits, snorkel gear and a new light wetsuit. I was prepared.

With the help of a sleeping pill and an open seat beside me, I slept much of the nine hour flight. Upon arriving, I met our local coordinator, who strung a lei around my neck, and the other six I-Helpers who had been on the flight. In our small group we had a man in his late twenties, a woman in her thirties, a couple with their thirteen year old daughter, and my roommate, a retired librarian from South Carolina. Since we dined together at our motel, I got to know them well as the week progressed.

Rarotonga strongly resembled Hilo, Hawaii where I had lived for six years. The greenery was lush with the same colorful plants – hibiscus, bougainvillea, heliconia, ginger, ti plants. The island circled around two sharp-peaked volcanos. A coral reef edged much of the seashore. To get around the island by public transportation, visitors had to take either the clockwise or "anti-clockwise" bus, as they called it, each of which ran only twice an hour. I spent a lot of time checking bus schedules and waiting for buses, not my fantasy of living in paradise.

The people of Rarotonga are Cook Islander Maori, a Polynesian group that speaks a language close to Hawaiian and Tahitian. Knowing a bit of Hawaiian, I enjoyed piecing Maori words together. Although, regrettably, I didn't get to meet many Maori people, except for service personnel in shops or restaurants, they seemed gentle and relaxed as most Pacific Islanders are.

Our group stayed at a motel fifteen minutes from town by bus. True to the photo from I-Helpers' website, the motel sat next to the ocean. Day and night I heard the surf thumping the shore. The problem was that between the motel and the water were rocks, sharp rocks, and no beach. To swim I had to take the bus to the lagoon, twenty minutes from the motel in the other direction.

Nonetheless, the sound of the surf was pleasing – about the only thing about the hotel that was. The rooms were large but shabby. Dresser drawers stuck from warped wood. The water in the sink and shower ran hot and cold, but the pipes were not connected, so my shower was either uncomfortably cold or too hot to bear. Worst of all, four or five irritating roosters roamed the grounds. They started crowing at five a.m. and never quit all day. Ear plugs failed to muffle their racket.

The team's meals took place in our motel meeting

room where I discovered another of the disadvantages of being in the remote Pacific. Except for fruit, salad, chicken and fish, everything else had to be shipped in from overseas which made non-local food such as cheese, yoghurt or wine costly. The motel cuisine was repetitive and uninteresting unless you like potato salad at every meal. Fortunately, the two times our team went out to dinner we had a tasty fish dinner and an Indian buffet. I kept thinking the program would have benefitted greatly from optional restaurant dinners for those willing to pay, but, since no one seemed willing to pay for a meal already included in our trip fee, I might have been eating alone.

While room and board were disappointing, I was excited to be assigned to teach ESL in the Learning Resource Center at the large high school on the island. The Center especially served athletic scholarship students from the outer islands who were semi-literate in English and definitely needed help. The students were generally tall, muscle-bound, and bright-eyed. School rules required that the girls tie up their bountiful locks and the boys keep their thick black curls above the collar.

On the first day, my fellow I-Helper volunteer and I were taught how to administer and score reading tests. This was a boring task usually performed by older student helpers. Back at the motel, I informed the I-Helper coordinator that I was hoping to teach ESL as advertised. She bristled, remarking I was there to do whatever the school needed and ESL was not a regular activity. From my room I brought her I-Helpers' printed information showing an ESL assignment. Although she shrugged me off, she apparently sent Rosie, the high school coordinator, an email saying I wasn't satisfied with my work.

The next morning when I arrived at school, Rosie suggested I take one of the students and teach him ESL.

"Fine," I said. "Where are the ESL materials?"

"We don't have any."

"Well, how do you expect me to teach?"

"Just make something up."

An experienced ESL teacher, I decided to give my

imagination a try. I picked up the book the student was assigned, a Harry Potter. It couldn't have been more inappropriate since my semi-literate student had a terrible time with the vocabulary and an even harder time imagining British street scenes. I gamely made up some multiple choice and fill-in-the-blank questions but the process was slow. At the end of an hour, the student went off to his class in Maori and I deposited the pad with my questions on the office table. It was gone the next day.

I believe I could have made a difference if I'd seen the same students for a couple of hours each day. Rosie indicated that was not possible, and so I gave up on creating an ESL program and went back to tutoring reading. Since the cottage that housed the Learning Resource Center was usually mobbed with noisy kids bouncing around the small space, I asked for a quieter place to work. I was given a corner of the porch, and it was pleasant sitting outdoors. I didn't get far, however, because the school had a long and early lunch break from 10:30 to 11:25 and another break from 1:00 to 1:30. We volunteers spent a lot of time sitting around doing nothing.

Our first couple of days had some sun and, after school, I took the bus to different beaches along the lagoon. The fish were practically identical to the fish I had come to know and love in Hawaii. It was wonderful to see a Humuhumunukunukuapua'a again. Although my guidebook had promised a dry winter season, the next couple of days were cloudy and gray with occasional outbursts of heavy rain. I spent an afternoon wandering around town, a small collection of tourist shops and cafes, and the rest of the time I read or napped in my room, trying to catch up on sleep regularly terminated by the crowing five a.m. wake-up call.

By the fifth day, I concluded I was neither giving nor getting much from the program. I decided to shorten my trip to one week and catch the direct flight to Los Angeles two days later. I worried about the cost of changing my ticket and finding a vacant seat, but one call to Air New Zealand and I was home free. While I'd paid a sizeable amount for my "volunteer" experience and was leaving halfway through, I couldn't imagine feeling useful or rewarded by a second week.

When I informed my I-Helpers coordinator I was leaving, she seemed rather perturbed.

"I'm sure next week will be better," she said, "when you are working with the women's group."

I'd already spent part of a day with the group. "I have to tell you," I replied, "that the group has nothing for me to do except observe their activities."

"You might learn a lot observing," she insisted.

I wasn't persuaded. I hadn't come all the way to the Cook Islands to be an observer. "You know, I think I can contribute more to the world right at home."

"Then I wish you a good trip. Of course, I'll give you a ride to the airport."

"That's great. Thank you."

On the flight home, the ticket agent gave me three seats to stretch across. It was heaven, the best sleep I'd gotten since the start of the trip.

As I reflected on my aborted volunteer experience, I felt disappointed it hadn't gone better. I thought long and hard about what I'd learned – about the program and myself.

With respect to my volunteer work, I concluded that dropping into another country's educational system and tutoring for a couple of weeks could not accomplish much, if anything. In contrast, a couple of librarians in my volunteer group, working in school libraries in abysmal shape, managed to sort and catalogue hundreds of books. Their work had a tangible outcome, rather like building a house in Habitat for Humanity's program. My assignment – filling in for a teacher's aide or tutoring Harry Potter – seemed unproductive by comparison.

Perhaps if I'd been able to work with the same students every day, using my own ESL materials and providing exercises and handouts, I could have taught new vocabulary and worked on basic grammar. Instead, my assignment was structured around fitting into the school's existing program. I must acknowledge the other volunteers were less disgruntled than I. They seemed willing to do whatever the schools asked as just part of the volunteer experience.

Beyond service, my other goal for the trip had been to immerse myself in a Pacific Island culture. Our group's coordinator, a New Zealander married to a Maori, offered us a small taste of island life – some commentary on the local style of doing things, a few words of Maori, a brief introduction to foods made from taro or seaweed. I wanted to know the islands' history. While we took a self-guided tour at the Rarotonga Museum (there was no one there to answer questions), I learned more from reading about Rarotonga <u>before</u> I came. I was also eager to find out about Cook Island politics but the coordinator and her husband said they stayed away from anything political. By asking questions, I did learn a bit about small problems of island life – the high cost of living, local resentment of New Zealanders and other foreigners who controlled the tourist economy, and competition for resources between

Rarotonga and the outer islands. I would have liked to know more.

I recognize my quest for more knowledge and cultural exposure stemmed from my academic and particular travel background. My fellow group members seemed satisfied with their introduction to Cook Island life. While the program was adequate for them, I longed for a way to interact with Maori people. I had thought such cultural exchange was built into my program, but realized I would have to reach out for it. That was hard to do from a motel far from the town center.

As for accommodations and leisure-time activities, I must reiterate the differences between the Web's presentations and the facts on the ground. From my Web research, I expected the motel to be attractive with snorkeling right off the beach. As noted, the motel was rundown and there was no beach, with the closest snorkeling a bus ride away. The Web and I- Helpers also informed me we would experience sunny winter weather with temperatures in the high 70s. As mentioned, during most of the week the sky was covered by billowing clouds and I was drenched by occasional downpours. I should have packed an umbrella.

Could I have done a better job relating to my team members? The most compatible people were a family and naturally tended to interact among themselves. The two younger singles were, in one case, depressed over a broken marriage and in the other, homesick after traveling and being away from home for two months. Finally, given our differences, I would never have chosen my room-mate – a right wing conservative and a chatterbox. Perhaps I should have paid for a single room, but it would have cost me another $450. I doubt peace and quiet in my room would have ben enough to make me stay a second week.

My last issue with I-Helpers was the cost, which was $2600 for two weeks and included room, board and local transportation but not overseas airfare. The organization, despite its service orientation, seemed to be taking in a fair amount of money. Since most of I-Helper's programs were in the same price range ($2600 to $2800 for two weeks),

I suspect the less costly programs like mine helped pay for the more expensive ones in Europe as well as considerable U.S. administrative overhead.

When I got back from my week in Rarotonga, I compared notes with a friend who had been on a considerable number of volunteer programs run by several different outfits. She had just returned from her first trip with I-Helpers, volunteering in Italy, and agreed that teaching English in a foreign school system was neither productive nor rewarding. On the other hand, she had had a lively cultural experience, meeting Italians in the village where she worked and food shopping at the school break with the Italian teacher she was assigned to. With her husband who was also a volunteer, she was able to make a number of side trips to nearby villages. Her group savored good Italian food and stayed in a pleasant hotel on the Adriatic. I regret I had none of the cultural pluses my friend enjoyed.

Would I ever go on another overseas volunteer activity? I remain tempted by the large variety of fascinating locales visited by different volunteer outfits. Before signing up, however, I would want to know ahead of time that my work experience would produce some kind of tangible outcome. Also, I would choose a place with a culture quite different from something I already knew. Although Rarotonga was lovely, it was too much like Hawaii, a place I knew well. Finally, I would choose either to travel with a friend or participate in a larger group of volunteers in order to have a wider selection of individuals with whom to interact.

The more I think about the Cook Islands, the more I realize I could have salvaged the experience if there had been other places to explore, as my friend did by visiting Italian villages. Since Rarotonga was so small, there were not many diversions. The closest other island was a flight away and the cost for a one-day tourist visit, including airfare and a boat trip, was $350, more than I was willing to pay to see another beautiful lagoon. If, instead of Rarotonga, I had volunteered in Italy, Portugal or Tanzania, I could have traveled during or after the experience and had a more interesting trip.

The best part of the Cook Islands experience for me was re-encountering the Pacific's glorious sea life. If I volunteer again in the future, I need to remember to choose carefully among the varieties of enticing fish in the sea.

One for the Road

Traveling alone evokes strong feelings for many people. They feel anxiety about loneliness – having no one with whom to share the travel experience, eating meals alone, going to sleep every evening without companionship. While extroverts can typically strike up conversations with strangers, shy people or introverts fear embarrassing themselves by approaching those they don't know. Along with anxiety comes fear about managing on one's own – obtaining necessary information, finding appropriate lodging, getting lost, or encountering personal danger. I recall often panicking over the location of my passport until I got a fanny pack and always zipped it up in the same compartment.

Yet others feel enthused about traveling on their own. They are heady about the personal freedom they have on the road, anticipate making new acquaintances, and feel challenged by the idea of reaching out to others. For many years, I was one of those. In my thirties and forties, I often traveled alone. I loved creating my own journeys and meeting both fellow travelers and inhabitants of other countries. Of course, I was at a good age for traveling alone – old enough to have learned from past travels, young and attractive enough to appeal to my peers, and just the right age to be comfortable with both younger and older generations.

Today, traveling alone is nowhere near as enticing. In my mid-sixties, "one for the road" means something quite different. I no longer mix easily with people much younger than I am. I struggle to handle heavy luggage by myself. I doubt I can outrun someone who appears threatening.

More important than any of these, however, is the sad fact that I am no longer traveling alone by choice. Losing my dear husband to sudden cardiac arrest made me an involuntary single. Although, at the time Jim died, he was less interested in travel than I was, I could always count on him to come along if his company was something I sorely wanted. We had planned a trip to Greece for September, 2010, five months after Jim passed away. While taking that trip was hard for me because Jim and I shared so much of Greece together, it was also comforting to maintain a bond with our Greek friends – even if I was alone.

One for the road. I have reflected on ways to make that journey. It would be lovely to travel with a friend – as long as it was the right friend. I would not want to be with someone addicted to daily tourism. I prefer a deeper connection to places than sightseeing. I want to feel a place and taste it and smell it rather than merely see it. I also prefer not to travel with someone who has personal traits or patterns that are difficult for me – a night owl, a snorer, a cheapskate, an obsessive shopper. While I'm prepared to tolerate others' ways, I don't want to keep feeling irritated. And, as I learned on my visit to San Miguel, it is not easy as a single to travel with a married couple. For all these reasons, it may be challenging to find the right fellow traveler.

An alternate to traveling with a companion is to go with a group. Yet it might also be difficult to find the right group. I have no interest in seeing ten cities in twenty days. Nor am I enthusiastic about groups of seniors; I prefer being with people of all ages. A number of my friends take "adventure tours," which intrigue me because they emphasize interaction with local culture. I have checked out these trips, however, and they seem rather pricey, perhaps because I spent many years organizing such trips without taking a fee. Friends have urged me to go back to leading women's groups, but I know, from 30 years' experience, that creating my own groups and leading them is arduous. I no longer desire such hard work to cover travel costs.

Perhaps the greatest disincentive is that group

members tend to interact with each other, rather than with the people whose land they are visiting. For me, the worst such experience would be a cruise in which group members are constantly thrown together on a ship and, when they disembark, enjoy only a day-long, whirlwind tour. Engaging with locals happens most easily when the visitor joins a local group. That's what happened when I traveled with American high school students to France, lived for a month with a French family, and ended the summer on a camping trip with French and American students. Oh, to be 17 again.

Since I'm no longer a backpacker or hostel voyager, single travel will be somewhat more costly for a middle aged, middle class woman rooming alone. Despite my reservations about traveling with a companion or group, a shared room or a group tour bus would cost less than being by myself. At the same time, some of my particular travel modes might be more economical than traveling with a friend or group. I'm perfectly happy to stay in a room with a bathroom down the hall or to book second class on trains. I don't need three large meals a day as are typically served to groups. Thus, the expenses of being a single but traveling in my own style might even out.

I suspect that, for the foreseeable future, I will be happiest traveling alone. Certainly, there are ways to make "one for the road" easier, such as returning to places where I already know locals, hoping, of course, they will be happy to see me again. While it often consumes a lot of time to plan a trip and make sure your acquaintances will be available, it is rewarding to return for at least some of a journey to a place I know and people I like.

If the goal, however, is to go someplace new and meet new people, one way to do so is with a little-known program called Servas, which means "we serve" in Esperanto. The organization seeks to foster peace, good will and mutual respect by connecting people from different countries through home stays. Started by pacifists at the end of World War II, Servas today encompasses more than 15,000 homes in more than 125 countries. Membership means hosting or visiting other Servas members for a couple of nights and providing or receiving a person-to-person introduction to the community.

Jim and I joined Servas before our trip to New Zealand in 2008. In Auckland, we stayed with a delightful Servas couple for two nights. We learned about their occupations, families, and many previous Servas visitors. They gave us tours in the countryside and took us for a picnic at their favorite winery. They even offered to pick us up at the airport! Today, when I consider taking off on my own, especially to Europe which has many Servas members, I welcome the idea of re-connecting to Servas.

While my travel options are more limited than thirty years ago, I still relish the thought of journeying around the world. Travel enriches my life by awakening my senses. My ongoing taste for another land is sharper when I discover the piquant flavors of its herbs and spices. My antennae vibrate when I actually hear drums beating in the countryside. My nostrils quiver when, on a Metro, I smell the musky odor of the crowds. Even at home, my past travel experiences bring vitality to what I read, watch on film, or discuss, vibrant colors to the black and white world.

In the introduction, I described a journey as a passage from ignorance to enlightenment. To keep growing and learning, sensing and feeling, I've got to devise itineraries, pack my suitcase, zip up my passport, and go.

I certainly hope to meet you somewhere along the road.